Journey from Anxiety to Freedom

Journey from Anxiety to Freedom

*Moving Beyond
Panic and Phobias
and Learning to Trust Yourself*

Mani Feniger

PRIMA PUBLISHING

PRIMA PUBLISHING and colophon are registered trademarks of Prima Communications, Inc.

Disclaimer

Prima Publishing has designed this book to provide information in regard to the subject matter covered. It is sold with the understanding that the publisher and the author are not liable for the misconception or misuse of information provided. Every effort has been made to make this book as complete and as accurate as possible. The purpose of this book is to educate. The author and Prima Publishing shall have neither liability nor responsibility to any person or entity with respect to any loss, damage, or injury caused or alleged to be caused directly or indirectly by the information contained in this book. The information presented herein is in no way intended as a substitute for medical counseling. Although the following stories are true, some of the names have been changed to respect the privacy of individuals and their families.

Library of Congress Cataloging-in-Publication Data

Feniger, Mani.
    Journey from anxiety to freedom: moving beyond panic and phobias and learning to trust yourself / Mani Feniger.
        p.   cm.
    ISBN 0-7615-0860-0
    1. Anxiety—Popular works. 2. Panic disorders—Popular works.
3. Phobias—Popular works. 4. Self-help techniques. I. Title.
    RC531.F46 1996
616.85'22—dc20   96-33369
                                                                          CIP

            99 00 01 HH 10 9 8 7 6 5 4 3
Printed in the United States of America

How to Order:

Single copies may be ordered from Prima Publishing, P.O. Box 1260BK, Rocklin, CA 95677; telephone (916) 632-4400. Quantity discounts are also available. On your letterhead, include information concerning the intended use of the books and the number of books you wish to purchase.

Visit us online at http://www.primapublishing.com

With gratitude to Alice and Jacob.

Contents

Foreword

It is estimated that nearly a quarter of the adult population of the United States will have an anxiety disorder at some point in their lives. Over thirty million people in this country alone have some form of anxiety that severely curtails their freedom and enjoyment of life. Despite these huge figures, anxiety disorders are often unrecognized, misunderstood, or misdiagnosed. Too often people suffering from general anxiety, panic disorder, or phobias live with overwhelming fear. Some of them become frustrated and depressed, convinced that they are incurable or doomed to a limited, unfulfilling life.

No one should have to continue to live in such extreme discomfort when we now have the tools and treatments to provide relief and freedom from debilitating anxiety. Recognizing the epidemic proportions of anxiety-related conditions, the Anxiety Disorders Association of America (ADAA), in conjunction with the National Institute of Mental Health (NIMH), has mounted a broad educational campaign to educate the general public as well as the medical and mental health community about these conditions. Several organizations collaborate to sponsor National Anxiety Disorders Screening Day at the beginning of May each year so that anyone can get a free screening and information.

In the current climate of greater acceptance and communication about painful personal issues, more and more people are finding the courage to speak out about their challenges and to ask for support. However, although many insurance plans and health care facilities offer medication, they sometimes fail to provide the specialized educational and cognitive-behavioral programs that give patients and clients the proven, practical tools to manage anxiety and panic disorders and free themselves from limiting phobias. A lot of progress has been made over the last ten years, but too many people are still without an effective recovery plan that takes into account their personal learning style and particular emotional needs.

Journey from Anxiety to Freedom is a book that had to be written. It fills the information gap by offering clear, simple explanations, techniques, and exercises to alleviate panic and anxiety. These are presented through the perspectives of eight people from different walks of life. This is not only a book of facts; it contains the stories of real people who have learned specific skills and attitudes that changed their lives. I am one of the people you will meet in this book. You will most likely find among us somebody who speaks directly to your own experience.

I have found that learning from your peers is especially helpful in facing fears and learning to trust yourself. We don't hesitate to tell a friend or associate if we have a back problem, or to call a physical therapist to ask about exercises to relieve physical pain or stress. But our culture has put a stigma on issues related to mental or psychological health, as though these topics are too unique or too private to talk about. Every person—doctor, lawyer, mother, father, teacher, computer programmer—has emotional and psychological challenges. That's part of being human. If you have been uncomfortable discussing your fears, you will be relieved to find people like you who are ready to reveal their experience and serve as an inspiration for you.

The level of personal engagement in this book reminds me of the quality of support and contact that occurs in the Phobease classes I teach. Connection to others is vital for people struggling with anxiety because for too long each of us has thought we were the only one suffering. It is time to remove this misconception by meeting other people—creative, respected, effective, sensitive, courageous people—who have faced their fears and moved on to live joyous, fulfilling lives.

Another benefit of this book is that you will be introduced to several different treatment options that will give you a sense of the range of possibilities you have to choose from. You don't have to fit yourself into a single narrow technique that many not be suited to you; you can experiment with any combination of approaches that appeals to you and adjust your personal program as you go along.

Journey from Anxiety to Freedom presents a map and a pathway of hope and relief for the millions of people who are ready and eager to proceed on their journey of living fully. Bon voyage!

—Howard Liebgold, M.D., founder of the Phobease Program and author of *Curing Phobias, Shyness, and Obsessive Compulsive Disorder*

Acknowledgments

As I think about all the people who have contributed to *Journey from Anxiety to Freedom,* I am amazed and humbled by the generosity and commitment of so many wonderful human beings. The heart of this book is the truth-telling of the men and women whose lives are described here. *Journey from Anxiety to Freedom* was completed because of the friends and associates who believed it was important and gave emotional support and expertise during years of interviewing and writing. Although I spent many hours sitting alone at my computer, this book is a testament to community, collaboration, and generosity of spirit.

First I want to express my love and gratitude to Lianne Obadia, the Writer's Midwife, for her intuition, skillfulness, and years of dedication to every phase, from conception to final editing. My deepest appreciation goes to Marcia Dickman for her dauntless commitment to find just the right word; to Naomi Lucks, whose professional judgment gave me the confidence to go on; to Howard Liebgold, who always said yes; to

Loie Rosenkrantz for her loving, wise counsel; to Fawn Moran for her vision; to Sucheta Frankel, who always showed up at just the right time; to Diane Mintz for her attention to details; to Gaila Marie Allen for her sensitivity; to Dale Ireland for being such a light; to Tricia Dolter for her inspirational telephone calls; to Loretta Valentine for transcribing the interviews; to Patricia Allison for her caring comments; to Denver Coleman and Theresa Tollini-Coleman for being role models of creative perseverance; to Selene Kramer for her infinite compassion; and to Mano Collinge for her humor and thousands of cups of tea.

Many friends and acquaintances encouraged me, read manuscripts, shared their experiences, and contributed in more ways than I can enumerate here. I am grateful to Narayan Luke Anderson, Ian Arion, Steve Baczewski, Sherry Burkart, Lynette Chambers, Gary Covazos, Jane Ehrlich, Gale Entrekin, Rachel Gila, Landes Good, Roberta Gould, Robin Gurse, Bonnie Halpern, Terry-Linda Hodge, Kathy Indermill, Frank Jorgenson, Judith Claire Joy, Premsiri Khalsa, Lolli Levine, Sharda Miller, Susan Muth, Naresh, Susan Penzner, Deborah Rezente, Gyani Richards, Helen Schiffman, Raphael Shevelev, Henry Soltelo, Patrick Tribble and Catherine Valdez.

My gratitude forever goes to Hilda Perlowin for her no-nonsense guidance at 60 MPH. For offering their expertise in treating anxiety disorders: Jackie Grey, Joyce Kaplan, Howard Liebgold, Sita Packer, Tom Rucker, and Kathie Weston. For their invaluable programs, I want to acknowledge the late Dr. Arthur

Hardy, founder of TERRAP; David Quigley, founder of the Alchemical Hypnotherapy Institute; and Jeru Kabbal, founder of the Institute for Accelerated Personal Transformation.

I'd like to express my appreciation to the people who generously gave me advice about the publishing process: Renee Baron, Sue Bender, Ernest Callenbach, William Collinge, Zipporah Collins, Mark Copithorne, Judy Hardin, Marcia Perlstein, Elizabeth Wagele, Dorothy Wall, and Patrice Wynne. Special thanks to my agent, Leslie Keenan, for her unwavering confidence in this book, and to the staff at Prima, especially Acquisitions Editor Georgia Hughes, Project Editor Debra Venzke, and Publicist Christine Lemmon. An author could not hope for a more considerate, communicative team.

I would like to thank Coleman Barks for permission to quote the Rumi excerpts from *Birdsong*, published by MAYPOP, and "Birdwings" from *The Essential Rumi* published by HarperCollins; and Dale Ireland for her poems.

Through these years of healing and writing, I have experienced a deepening of friendship and mutual respect with members of my family: my late uncle William Wedgewood; Tom and Harriet Feniger; Arlone and Wayne Gardner; Key; Monika; my daughter, Sarah, who has been a teacher and a light; and my partner, Michael, for his loving companionship, for seeing who I really am, and for great dinners. I thank the divine spirit which has blessed me and shown me that I am never alone.

Birds make great sky-circles
of their freedom.
How do they learn it?

They fall, and falling,
they're given wings.

—Excerpt from a quatrain of Rumi,
translated by Coleman Barks

Introduction

It's a sunny afternoon, cooled by a slight breeze blowing off San Francisco Bay. My attention is drawn to the movement of rustling leaves on the row of trees alongside the highway. Several cars speed by me in the left lane. They must be in a hurry to get somewhere. Not me. I am just here for the pleasure of the drive. I like being alone in my car, the solitude a relief after a busy week filled with people and appointments. I slip a Linda Ronstadt tape into the cassette player and hum along with a sentimental rendition of "What's New?" I see the upper towers of the Bay Bridge come into view, and soon after, the first strip of blue water. I say to myself, "I'll cross that bridge when I come to it." I smile.

Can this really be me?

I'm on the bridge now. A blue pickup pulls up close to my bumper. I notice it briefly in my rearview mirror and then turn my attention to what's in front of me. I say to myself, "Let the other guy take care of himself.

My domain is driving *this* car, not concerning myself
with how the other person wants me to drive." I continue at fifty-five, and the driver of the pickup pulls out
into the next lane and speeds on his way. I look ahead
and see I'm halfway across the bridge. I don't wish I
were already over to the other side or home in my living room. I say to myself, "Here I am, my hands on the
steering wheel, hearing the background hum of highway sounds, smelling the mild scent of the air drifting
through my open window, breathing this breath. This is
the only place I need to be right now, here, just here."

Can this really be me?

The other people on the road may not think what I'm
doing is special. They're busy going to work or to the
beach or to pick up their kids at school. Maybe they're
thinking about what to make for dinner or whether the
report got filed. They may not appreciate how much it
means to me to be able to do a mundane thing like
drive my car down the highway and across the bridge.
That's because they don't know that I once was overwhelmed by panic attacks, ashamed even to tell my
friends and family that I was too apprehensive to go
out. They don't know that this very dilemma guided me
toward the real experience of freedom—not just being
able to drive and fly again, but the freedom that comes
from loving and accepting myself.

Before I began my healing journey, my idea of
freedom was concrete and specific. If I could drive my
car to San Francisco, then I would be free to live again.
If I could go to work without being afraid that some

unexpected situation would cause me to panic, then I would be able to love myself again. I had maintained my responsibilities, even when the commute to work took more fortitude than the job itself. But on the inside I was withdrawing further into a shell, hoping to protect myself from the humiliation of exposing my unexplainable episodes of terror. The feelings of isolation and despair increased as avoidance and secrecy distorted my relationships. I didn't even tell my family in New York why I stopped visiting them. My life felt so constricted that I often felt I didn't have enough room to breathe.

I wanted so badly to be free. Deep down in my soul I must have known that I was yearning for a deeper freedom that wasn't measured by my daily performance. I must have dreamed of having a more enduring peace within myself that would sustain me through hard times as well as good times. But I was in crisis, physically and emotionally, and my immediate concern was to be able to function in the everyday situations of my life.

After five years of battling alone with my anxiety and watching my dread spread from one situation to another, I could no longer live with my own lies and excuses. The turning point came unexpectedly, after I received an invitation to my nephew's wedding. I stared at the reply card for a week, then finally called my brother on the East Coast. "I'm not coming to your son's wedding," I said, blushing with shame even though he couldn't see me. "It's not really because I don't have the time or the money. The truth is, I can't fly." I had finally said it out loud. I held my breath and waited.

After a moment's silence, my brother spoke, his voice softer than before. He encouraged me to tell him more about my life. When I finished my story of acute distress in cars and in elevators, of not wanting to travel or go too far from home, he gave me the news I had been waiting so long to hear. "You're not crazy," he said. "I've heard of this before. The experiences of fright you're describing are called panic attacks, and it sounds like you've developed some phobias. A close friend of ours had a similar problem; she didn't know how to prevent her panic reaction so she stopped going out with us. Once she understood what it was and got some help, she got so much better that she was able to take a job thirty miles from her home. The therapist she worked with has since moved to San Francisco. Would you like me to get her number?"

Telling the truth was the beginning of my healing. It helped me rebuild closeness to people who cared about me and to find the professional help I needed. I learned that the rush of disorienting sensations I experienced during a panic attack was triggered by an over-reaction of my body's emergency distress system, and that I could do something to change this response. For the first time I had a language and framework for looking at my fears. By working with the therapist my brother had recommended, I learned specific skills to reduce this panic reaction and cope more effectively with fear.

The road to mastering these skills required patience and perseverance. In time I was able to trust my anxiety-reducing skills and once again to feel safe being by myself, whether driving on freeways and bridges, taking elevators, or even flying. In 1992 I fulfilled a lifelong dream I had once written off as impossible. I flew to New Delhi and spent six weeks traveling with my husband in northern India. With each triumph, I experienced a feeling of exhilaration that I called "freedom." Yet even my definition of freedom changed as I integrated my growing list of victories into a new understanding of myself.

The challenge of panic has taken me on a journey I couldn't have imagined in the days when anxiety cast a shadow over all my experience. My healing process has given me a conscious way to approach any new challenge or opportunity, as well as a new perspective on what it means to be free. My experiences over these past ten years have shown me that freedom is more profound than merely the ability to fly or to drive. It is more enduring than the momentary sense of elation I get from performing well or the feeling of inadequacy when my insecurities are exposed. My real bridge to freedom is not made of steel. It is a bridge within myself, an attitude that takes me over the chasm of self-rejection to the peace of mind that comes with accepting myself and my life.

Contrary to what I had believed during the years I lived in torment about my "irrational" feelings, I discovered that I wasn't alone. Most people had some experience that they could relate to my distress. Wherever I went—to a party, professional event, or dinner engagement—the mere mention of my process of healing from panic and phobias elicited a similar account from someone else. All the stories I heard, whether they were about speaking in public, having a common medical procedure such as a mammogram, or going on a trip, included the same basic components: anticipation with dread, strange and disquieting physical symptoms, and frightening thoughts or feelings.

"Your phobia about bridges sounds like the feeling of dread I get whenever I'm about to go somewhere new." Or . . .

"I fly if I absolutely have to for business, but I'm in a sweat and white-knuckling it all the way." Or . . .

"I had to refuse that promotion. Even though I really know my material, my knees turn to jelly at the thought of presenting a report to the board of directors."

It hurt me to see other people suffering with a condition that I knew could be altered with the proper information and support. I realized that few of them understood what part they played in creating the cycle of rising anxiety that can lead to panic. They didn't know that worry and tension are often the result of learned mental and physical responses, or that with basic information and consistent practice these patterns can be changed. Many of the people I met assumed they had to tolerate living in constant discomfort. Some had lost their motivation to go after the things they wanted in their lives. It was painful to see people abandon their dreams, but most of all I couldn't bear to see lovely, capable, caring, decent human beings hate themselves as I once had.

I wrote *Journey from Anxiety to Freedom* because I know what it is like to live with debilitating fear. My first priority is to clearly present the proven, effective tools and practical suggestions for reducing anxiety, preventing panic, and curing phobias. Yet my intention is to go further than just showing you how to cope with fear. This book will also provide insights to help you heal the wound that stems from rejecting a part of yourself.

I gathered information for *Journey from Anxiety to Freedom* from many sources. I became an expert by consulting with others in the field of anxiety disorders, reviewing the books currently on the market, and attending several treatment programs including TER-RAP (an acronym for "Territorial Apprehension") and Phobease. I incorporated the wisdom gained through my own healing process, as well as my experience in professional practice as a counselor and hypnotherapist. My goal was to find a balance between objective, factual material and subjective, personal disclosure.

When I asked myself what had helped me most, I concluded that my greatest inspiration came from ordinary people who had dealt with similar fears. With that in mind, I chose to write this book not from the vantage point of the therapist describing her clients, but as another human being walking a parallel road. I also wanted to offer an alternative to reliance on medical or psychiatric experts as the ultimate authority, which I feel has contributed to feelings of dependency and powerlessness among patients and clients. I believe we each hold within us the power to heal ourselves and the ability to teach others from our own experience.

I interviewed many people, some who were in the midst of struggling with deep fear, others who had

achieved a high degree of freedom from panic and phobias. Of the dozens I interviewed, I was especially
drawn to seven individuals because of their openness,
their commitment to living fully, and their hope that
their experience could benefit others. I consider these
men and women members of my support team. I
thought you would want them on yours.

Journey from Anxiety to Freedom has two sections.
In Part I you will read what it was like to be immobi-
lized by fear, living with a secret and not knowing
where to turn for help. I won't spare you the hard times
people went through, because you probably have faced
hard times yourself. In chapter 3 you will witness them
as they turn a corner and embark on their healing journey. In chapters 4 through 8 you can accompany them,
day by day, step by step, as they learn specific techniques to cope with panic and reclaim the territory that
had been usurped by fear. You will hear how they put
their new skills into practice, and discovered that what
once required enormous effort could finally be done
with ease. You can look through their eyes and learn
from their stories in a natural way, as one benefits from
listening to a friend.

Part II will take you beyond the mechanics of alle-
viating panic to discovering the real spirit of freedom.
You will see pieces of a puzzle come together as your
new acquaintances uncover the roots of their anxiety
and self-judgment. They will invite you to share not just
the experiences of body and mind, but the spiritual
healing that comes through examining and changing
the limiting rules and beliefs that have been ingrained

since childhood. You will get a glimpse of what it is like to be free—free from debilitating fear, free from self-recrimination. You will get a taste of the rewards of their journey—self-discovery, growing trust, and gratitude for simple, ordinary pleasures.

We cross many bridges in a lifetime. For you the challenge may not be the Bay Bridge or the freeway. It may be speaking in public, becoming intimate with another person, or overcoming your fear of potential illness. It may be going to new places alone, taking airplanes, or attending classes. Whether you are dealing with the intense terror associated with panic or a gnawing anxiety that makes you dread specific occasions or experiences, you will find in *Journey from Anxiety to Freedom* the encouragement, support, and skills to take back command of your life. I hope you will discover that embracing the challenge of anxiety, panic, or phobias is not a detour on your journey but rather a path that guides you home to yourself.

Personal Profiles

Let me introduce you to the seven people (besides myself) whom you will meet in this book. These brief descriptions will highlight some of the difficulties we faced and the turning point that propelled us on the journey from anxiety to freedom.

Howard was voted California Physician of the Year, but often doubted his own value because he suffered from severe claustrophobia. He was too uneasy to sit in a movie theater, have a partner on the dance floor, or lecture in front of a class . . . *until he saw a feature story on the evening news that described his condition and the skills that could change his life.*

Bonnie became panic-stricken on a ski lift, and, because of her fear of heights, she avoided college courses that were located on high floors. She was so afraid of being labeled crazy that she kept her panic attacks a secret even from her husband . . . *until she found some books in a library that described her experience and led her to a home study cassette program for reducing anxiety.*

Edward covered up his dread of driving by working and living within a two-mile radius of his home. He kept small bottles of alcohol in his glove compartment to medicate himself enough to drive short distances . . . *until he realized that the alcohol was destroying his nerves, and he started attending A.A. Soon after, he found a group program for people with panic disorders and phobias.*

Kathy did her best to deal with some stressful family situations, but her panic episodes worsened over several years. She often was too anxious to go out— even to her front yard—and began to feel like a prisoner in her own home . . . *until an understanding doctor listened to her story, sent her a workbook to start her on a recovery program, and encouraged her with weekly phone consultations.*

Brian, the son of a commercial airline pilot, froze in terror during a routine flight to visit his family. After that, he lost his self-confidence and isolated himself from friends and professional acquaintances. When he canceled his planned vacation to Europe, he became withdrawn and depressed . . . *until he saw an ad in* Consumer Reports *and ordered a pamphlet describing the symptoms of anxiety disorder.*

Alicia was extremely uncomfortable speaking in social situations or making eye contact. When she took time off to get away from a stressful job, her fear of being embarrassed in front of others began to take over her life. She refused invitations and could hardly talk on the telephone . . . *until a chance conversation made her aware of a group where she could meet others with similar fears.*

Claire tried to cope with her catastrophic thoughts and frequent panic attacks by making elaborate plans to avoid the places she feared. She couldn't complete an MRI exam ordered by her doctor and depended on her husband to take her everywhere she needed to go . . . *until her determination to get help forced her medical plan to refer her to a therapist who worked specifically with panic disorders.*

Part I

Building a New Foundation

Section I

Coming to Awareness

1

Caught Off Guard

Fear has always been with me. As a child I was often afraid—of the teenagers I passed on my way to school, of riding the New York subway by myself, of staying alone in our big, creaky house, even when my aunt and uncle were upstairs in their flat. Since voicing my concerns didn't seem to gain me love or understanding, I learned to hold my breath and keep my fearful monologues to myself.

This way of coping didn't make my fear go away. Instead, scary thoughts I couldn't express turned into catastrophic scenes in my mind. I used my vivid imagination to foresee the worst possibilities and then I waited, tense and watchful, for something terrible to happen. I know now that my attempts to manage my fear eventually led to chronic inner anxiety. Even when I outgrew some of my childhood fears and became more self-assured, I often felt a vague, undefined apprehension, as though anticipating something I couldn't name or control.

Despite this apprehension, I managed to pursue a spirited life. My motivation was so strong that I kept going even with a knot in my stomach. I compensated for the fear by developing my intellect, creativity, and leadership abilities. I was vice-president of my high school, went out of town to college when I was just sixteen, traveled in Europe, and, after living in Italy for a year, returned to teach first grade in an underprivileged neighborhood in New York City. A few years later I married an artist and moved to a small cottage on the rugged coast of Maine. To others it appeared as though I was adventurous and independent. Indeed, that is how I saw myself, until a few incidents in my early thirties caught me completely off guard.

My Story: Overwhelmed by Fear

I was divorced and living with my eight-year-old daughter, Sarah, in California. I had promised to pick up a girlfriend, who was returning from spending the Christmas holidays in Paris. I piled Sarah and her overnight guest into the back seat of my old blue Valiant and drove to the freeway. It had rained on and off all day, and when I was almost to the airport, a sudden cloudburst covered my windshield with a sheet of water. Barely able to see the car in front of me, I turned my wipers to high speed. A quick glance at my watch told me that it was time for my friend's plane to land. When I looked back up at the road, everything seemed to be coming at me at once: the dizzying motion of the wiper blades, the glare of headlights striking the windshield, the roar as a truck barreled past, throwing a wall of water against my car.

For a moment I became confused, uncertain if I was still in my own lane. My heart pounded as my foot frantically reached for the brake pedal. The pedal didn't seem solid. I could hear Sarah and her schoolmate laughing in the back seat. Gripping the wheel, I sat up stiffly and used all my will to keep control of the car. Somehow I made it over to the exit ramp and into the parking garage. I was still trembling when my friend met us in the terminal. Even though she had just returned from a ten-hour flight, I told her I had flu symptoms and asked her to drive us back to my house. Though the experience upset me tremendously, I did my best to put it behind me. I went about my life as usual, but I couldn't help feeling more reluctant to drive on rainy nights.

Six months later, during a very stressful time, I went on a short vacation for a change of scene. When I fastened my seat belt in the airplane, I felt a tremor of fear start at my feet and vibrate through my whole body. I had an urge to run to the exit door, but I felt paralyzed. As the plane started down the runway, I turned to the person sitting next to me and asked for help. It seemed to me that I survived the short flight only through the kindness of this grandmotherly passenger who held my trembling hand during take-off and then chatted with me until I regained my equilibrium.

Although other disturbing incidents occurred over the next few years, I couldn't see any obvious pattern to my outbursts. I realized I was operating at an increasingly high level of daily stress, yet I did not know how to interpret the messages my body was giving me. Then, in 1980, I suffered a traumatic episode I couldn't digest and couldn't dismiss.

I was thirty-five years old at the time, working forty hours a week to provide for my daughter and myself. Sarah and I had been living in a small apartment in San Francisco since coming out from the East Coast, and had just moved in with a friend across the bay, who had a spacious home with a garden and deck overlooking the East Bay hills. There was nothing unusual about the day I got into my new housemate's red Datsun to go shopping with her, although I was exhausted from handling all the details of the move. As Linda's car picked up speed going down the hill, my heart started pounding and I jammed my feet up against the dashboard to stop the feeling of rushing headlong into space. For a split second I thought, "I'm going to explode. I'm going to die!" I screamed at Linda to slow down. Then, unable to respond to my friend's perplexed look, I withdrew into an embarrassed silence.

I didn't know what had happened. It had no name, no context. From that moment on I felt different, as though suddenly confronted with something that had been set loose in myself, something I couldn't control.

How Could This Happen to Me?

It wasn't until many years later that I finally learned that I was suffering from panic attacks. When they first started I didn't know what a panic attack was or how to manage my reaction. My stomach would tense whenever the memory of that terrible outburst in Linda's car entered my thoughts. I was sweaty and miserable whenever I was a passenger, even when the driver was someone I knew and had always felt safe with. Over time, my dread of *those feelings* came up even when I was doing the driving. Taking the freeway or going across local bridges became a gut-wrenching battle.

I found myself constantly imagining things that could go wrong. "What if I lose control and there's no one to help me?" "What if I can't breathe?" "What if . . . ?" I became increasingly wary about going places or entering situations I might not be able to leave easily if I felt the need to escape. In spite of my anguish, I tried to cope on my own. I didn't perceive my behavior as something that could be understood and changed. I wasn't aware that I could learn step-by-step skills to work with my anxiety. I thought it was just some awful part of me I had to live with. The best I could do was to get to my job, be a responsible parent, and fabricate excuses to explain why I often declined to go places or do things.

Panic can be especially disconcerting, even shocking, because it commonly strikes during an ordinary, everyday activity you've done a thousand times: going shopping, standing in line, driving your car. It can also occur upon waking from sleep, when you find your heart pounding yet have no reference for what precipitated it. The very ordinariness of the places in which my experiences of severe panic occurred made me feel confused and ashamed. With no earthquake or robbery to justify the pounding of my heart, I became uncertain of my ability to keep my composure in familiar, everyday situations.

In hindsight I can see that although the situation was commonplace, my extreme reaction in Linda's car happened at a time when I was feeling physically exhausted and emotionally stretched. I felt guilty that my daughter had to leave her friends and change schools. I was getting more deeply involved in a significant, personal relationship, the first since my divorce five years earlier. I had a longer commute to work. I wasn't thinking of all these changes when I got in the car to buy some kitchen supplies, but now I understand how they contributed to what happened that day.

No one can say with certainty why the nervous system produces a panic reaction on one occasion and not another. However, increasing evidence indicates that certain conditions may make one more susceptible. A crisis or period of increased stress may set the stage for your nervous system to work overtime. A change in circumstances, the death or illness of someone close to you, an operation or accident, moving, having a baby, changing jobs, or an emotional blow that affects your sense of security can make you more vulnerable to panic. Cumulative factors, each in itself not particularly significant, may also increase the likelihood of a panic attack. You may handle each individual problem without realizing that you have begun to operate from a consistently high level of anxiety.

Panic does not necessarily occur at the time you are in crisis. Sometimes fear gets stored away, as in the case of survivors of wars or of childhood abuse, until some association or problem brings it back up to the surface. In these cases, the panic response may be a symptom of post-traumatic stress. Regardless of when panic occurs, the characteristics of the panic response are fairly consistent, although the particular symptoms may vary from person to person.

Anatomy of a Panic Attack: The Body-Mind Connection

A panic attack generally starts with some restlessness or agitation, sweaty palms, dry mouth, or butterflies in the stomach. People often report a rise in body heat or a feeling of iciness, a tight chest, difficulty breathing or swallowing, trembling, a nervous bowel, or a racing heart. As panic symptoms become more intense, they can include visual distortions such as seeing objects or people as strangely distant or out of focus. Symptoms like feeling upside down or not quite on your feet, having a sense of impending doom, or feeling numb or disconnected from your body are also possible in the panic state. These feelings are often accompanied by thoughts that you're going crazy, about to do something dangerous, or even that you're having a heart attack or dying. No one has all of these symptoms at once, although a panic attack is defined as including at least four of them.

Stress is part of our lives, and physical sensations such as sweaty palms or butterflies in the stomach are a natural part of our body's response to our thoughts and feelings. However, in a classic panic attack, sensations may rapidly escalate from discomfort to an almost overwhelming intensity accompanied by catastrophic thoughts. When I learned more about the mechanics of the panic response, I discovered that with awareness and tools, we can intervene during the early stages of anxiety and stop the escalation of sensations before they develop into a full-blown panic attack. Without this understanding, a stricken person may feel caught off guard and remain shaken and disoriented, sometimes long after the actual physical panic subsides.

To understand the dynamics of a panic attack, we must look deeper than the external situation to find the internal mechanism that triggers the anxiety or panic reaction. The panic cycle usually starts with a frightening thought. This may be a "What If" thought or a "What People Think" (WPT) thought: "What if the car keeps picking up speed on the hill and goes out of control?" "What if they hear my voice quaver when I speak in front of the group?" All people have worry thoughts. But for some people, particularly those with a rich imagination and a sensitive nervous system, these thoughts, even when subconscious, can stimulate intense emotional and physiological responses.

Once the mind registers a frightening thought, it sends an alarm signal to the adrenal gland. Adrenalin, known as the "fight or flight" hormone, causes the autonomic nervous system to accelerate the heart rate and withhold blood from the skin and digestive organs so it is available to increase muscle tension in readiness for action. A whole sequence of involuntary physical adjustments prepares the body to respond with magnified strength, alertness, and speed. Like caffeine or alcohol, adrenalin works like a drug and has a cumulative effect in the bloodstream. The more hormone secreted, or the faster it is accumulated, the more radical its effect.

This emergency response system is extremely valuable when you are faced with a physical threat. If the house is on fire and you need to run for your life, or you must lift a two-ton truck off a child's leg, the rush of extra adrenalin and several accompanying stress chemicals is appropriately utilized by the body. The problem arises when the emergency reaction is triggered by an anticipated physical danger or a perceived psychological blow. The nervous system registers our fear of rejection, disapproval, humiliation, or loss of control, and our chemistry responds in the same way it would to actual physical assault.

Our brain cannot always distinguish a real threat from an imagined one. A negative thought, image, or even a shift in body language such as increased muscle tension, may send the signal to secrete adrenalin, setting into motion the chemical changes needed for fight or flight. Small amounts of adrenalin cause an increase in breathing rate or a queasy stomach—things we associate with being nervous. A larger or sudden discharge into the bloodstream sets off a temporary imbalance and may stimulate the physiological changes that we call a panic attack.

Without tools to interrupt this body-mind feedback loop, we can set in motion a cycle of escalating fear. A thought or association, conscious or unconscious, sets off a false alarm signal. If we don't understand the sensations that are aroused, they may frighten us, and we start to think even more terrifying thoughts. "I'm having a heart attack." "I'm dying." "I'm going to faint . . . blow apart . . . lose control . . ." The body reacts to the next round of fearful thoughts and releases another burst of adrenalin.

Although everyone experiences fearful thoughts or negative self-talk at times, some of us may have a greater physical predisposition to react with a panic response. Recent studies indicate that a genetic factor may cause the tendency for panic to run in families. Right from birth, certain babies exhibit a more pronounced startle response, reacting to sounds and lights that leave other infants unperturbed. These same individuals may be more physiologically sensitive to all stimuli, including chemical substances such as caffeine, medications, or adrenalin. Although all people experience stress, some respond to stress by developing ulcers or headaches. Others are more vulnerable to the panic response.

Regardless of our physiological tendencies, understanding the connection between mind and body is the first step toward taking the mystery out of the experience of panic. The panic response is temporary, not life-threatening, and it can be stopped by preventing or reducing the flow of excessive adrenalin. As you will discover in subsequent chapters, we can affect our physical reaction by identifying and changing the anxiety-provoking, catastrophic thinking habits that contribute to the panic response and by learning to relax.

Evolution of a Phobia

Fear is a normal, essential part of human experience. It can make us more alert to a potential danger so we can assess the situation and respond effectively. In contrast, a *phobia* is defined as an *excessive* or *irrational* fear. Instead of helping us respond in a practical way to an object or situation, the intense visceral feelings associated with phobias cause us to react inappropriately or out of proportion to the actual circumstance. The most common phobias are *simple* or *single* phobias, associated with things such as insects, animals, blood, needles, water, heights, thunder, and lightning. You have probably heard the term arachnaphobia, fear of spiders, made famous by the movie of the same name. Many people have at least one simple phobia during the course of their lives. It may cause considerable distress if the object or situation is encountered or some inconvenience in the effort to avoid contact. But this type of phobia usually doesn't dramatically compromise one's overall functioning.

Phobias were not new to me. When I was a child, I was afraid of snakes, recoiling at the colored images in my storybooks. Even the entwined snakes on the medical caduceus symbol evoked an irrational feeling of terror. My response to snakes is typical of a simple phobia.

It was possible for me to stay away from snakes, but the terror I was beginning to feel in ordinary circumstances was not so easy to compartmentalize. Since I couldn't predict when panic would again arise, my dread began to spread to other milieus in which I felt restricted or imagined that I would become helpless if panic were to occur. My avoidance was typical of *territorial phobias*. My fear expanded to include freeways (especially driving in any lane other than the exit lane), tunnels, elevators, and airplanes. Other common sites for territorial phobias are shopping malls, enclosed spaces, heights such as balconies, or roads that border steep cliffs.

Although I had some concern about embarrassing myself, I did not dread social situations or suffer from the kind of social phobias you will hear described by other people in the book. *Social phobias* are more focused on the extreme discomfort aroused by being observed and the fear of being judged or ostracized by others. They are most often associated with interpersonal situations such as speaking in front of others, signing your name in public, using public restrooms, eating in restaurants, attending classes, making small talk, or having eye contact.

For some people, the feeling of dread and the attempt to avoid is not connected to any particular location or specific situation. *Agoraphobia,* which comes from the Greek word meaning "fear of the market-place," is the term used to describe a general condition of being afraid of the panic reaction itself. It is associated with being unable to be alone when away from a place or person who is considered the source of safety. In its worst case, agoraphobia can lead to a fear of leaving one's own home. Many people with agoraphobia continue to go out though they may limit their activities to a well-defined radius or "safety" zone.

A phobia can develop when we experience high anxiety or unpleasant sensations and then mistakenly identify the situation or environment as the source of those feelings. It is not the bridge, the freeway, or the view from the balcony that causes these sensations. It is our own internal triggers—our inner tensions, our thoughts and fears—that are responsible for our reaction. Once we fully understand this, we can learn skills that help us gradually return to the situations that have become intimidating.

Some people who experience panic attacks—or *panic disorder,* which is defined as having four or more panic attacks in a month—do not become phobic or preoccupied with fear. They continue to return to the situations in which panic occurred and in some cases find that the panic symptoms decrease naturally over time. But if the anxiety about panic becomes more threatening, the attempt to control distressing feelings can lead to a systematic withdrawal from important aspects of life.

My own fear became an obsession. I had to weigh every situation in my life against my concerns. Will I feel safe? Will I be able to control myself? What if . . . ? My life was not based on my preferences or desires. I felt as though I no longer had a choice. I always found some excuse to avoid driving, as though ordinary weather conditions—rain, clouds, even heat or cold—really made a difference. I had to consider too much traffic (feeling trapped) or too little traffic (feeling uncomfortable with so much open space). I found myself declining invitations and opportunities for fear that I wouldn't have control over my environment and, most of all, over myself. When I did go out, I couldn't enjoy what I was doing because I was preoccupied with wishing I were already back home.

My concern was no longer limited to specific occasions. I had woven anxiety into the fabric of my life. The constant worry and guilt led to exhaustion, depression, and a general loss of joy. My fear of panic was a heavy weight on my life. Assuming that I was different from other people made me feel lost and alone. I did not know where to turn for help.

Some of these feelings may be familiar to you. If you have been plagued by panic or apprehension you don't understand, or if you hold back from doing things because of anxiety, you may be relieved to know that people who struggle with panic, anxiety, and phobias respond well to education and treatment. In this decade there are more options for healing than ever before, and health professionals are significantly better trained to identify these conditions at an early stage and provide appropriate services.

May 2, 1994, was the first National Anxiety Disorders Screening Day. In major cities throughout the United States, people flocked to health centers, hospitals, and public auditoriums to see educational videos and hear about the symptoms of anxiety and the resources available. Many of the screening sites had a bigger turnout than expected and had to schedule additional meetings to accommodate all the inquiries. In chapter 4 you will learn of different approaches to healing and you can begin to examine available treatment options.

Fear is not our enemy. Our goal is not to become fearless, but to be able to respond to fear in a conscious and effective manner. With accurate information and support we can change the patterns that create unmanageable fear. National Institute of Mental Health statistics indicate that over ninety percent of people who have a problem with panic can get significant and lasting relief through a combination of education, professional guidance, and medication when indicated.

Getting a New Perspective

When I look back over my experiences of the last fifteen years, it's humbling to recall that I once felt so isolated that I didn't even talk about my pain. But I had no words for what I was experiencing and didn't really consider that there might be something I could *do* to change my behavior. I saw myself as weak and immature.

Since that time I have been grateful to discover that many other people who have faced this challenge have been able to rebuild their lives, sometimes even turning in a new direction. Once I was introduced to the basic skills for reducing anxiety and returning to the situations I had avoided, I began to appreciate the fresh perspectives that came from investigating my own habits and assumptions. I realized that my problem was also my opportunity to discover myself and to grow. My learning process has turned out to be enriching and exciting and has brought me to an understanding of myself and of freedom that goes much deeper than just being able to manage anxiety.

In the next chapters I will introduce you to seven people who have walked this path of healing from fear to freedom. Like myself, some of them struggled with panic and phobias before these issues were as well understood as they are today. Until they had access to the information and support they needed, they coped by making excuses while retreating from important areas of their lives. Their motivation to tell their stories without hiding the painful details or diminishing the joy of their successes comes from knowing the healing power of telling the truth. Their hope, and mine, is that you can take something from their experiences and use it to further your own healing process.

How About You?

The exercises that follow each chapter will help you become more aware of your own situation and practice the tools for recovery. You may do them as you read, or you may want to read ahead and come back to them after you have a broader perspective on the whole issue.

Start a journal or notebook that you can use to record the observations and discoveries you make about yourself as you read this book. As you pay more attention to your own behavior, you may be able to add more specific information to the exercises. Use your journal to complete the exercises.

1. Naming Stress Symptoms

What is your body's reaction to stress or fear? In your journal, list the physical sensations that you experience when you feel nervous or afraid (for example, sweaty palms, trembling legs). Continue to add to the list as you become more aware of the physical symptoms that are responses to fear.

1. _____
2. _____
3. _____

Observe Your Thoughts

List the thoughts you have when you get scared or nervous (for example, "I can never do it right." "Everyone will think I'm stupid.") Read over your list and put a star next to any sensations or thoughts that cause you enough discomfort to stop you from doing something.

1. _____
2. _____
3. _____

2. *Fear Triggers*

In your journal, start a list of things or situations that trigger fear in you. This may include situations you dislike, approach with extreme apprehension, or try to avoid. When you have made your list of things and situations, observe your physical sensations, emotional responses, and thoughts and fill in each category.

Situation	Physical	Emotional	Thought
Speaking in class	trembling knees dry mouth	fear embarrassment	They can see through me

1. _____
2. _____

2

Living
with a Secret

Many people who have panic attacks appear composed on the outside, while inside they feel like they're falling apart. One woman told me about struggling to maintain her self-control in her doctor's waiting room. "I was sitting there and I looked around and thought, 'No one knows I'm going to go crazy in about one minute. If they don't call me soon, I'm going to explode!'" She herself was amazed at how well her secret was kept. Many people with panic or phobias feel alone, drained by the constant adjustments and excuses they must make to cover up their fear.

Disguising Fear

I remember what it was like to live with my secret. Even with my closest friends, I felt that my extreme fear separated me from others. It was the early eighties, and everyone used popular clichés about "letting go" of control and "going with the flow." But I was suffering from panic. The idea of letting go was terrifying; what I wanted was something to hold on to. As in my childhood, I believed that I was having the wrong feelings. Because my circle of friends was a substitute family for me, because I depended on my peers for emotional nourishment, I learned to disguise my fear even among my closest friends.

It was the same in my professional life. As the sales rep for a large graphics firm, I thought I always had to appear self-confident and self-assured. When a business associate suggested we discuss a project over lunch, I felt bad about myself for making excuses to avoid getting in a taxi with him. A voice in my head berated me, "A grown woman shouldn't make this a problem." On one occasion I planned a sales call and forgot to ask the suite number in advance. Gripping the handrail, I barely survived the high-speed elevator ride to the thirty-fifth floor, only to be met by a designer who enthusiastically led me to the full-length picture windows. While pretending to enjoy the view, I averted my eyes and prayed that I wouldn't become hysterical then and there. Living with a secret takes constant vigilance.

Introducing Howard: Guarding His Secret

I met Dr. Howard Liebgold for the first time in his office at the hospital where he was head of the Department of Rehabilitation. His sparkling eyes, bright multicolored tie, and sense of humor immediately offset the formality associated with meeting a physician. Although he now teaches classes on curing phobias, his original area of study was not psychology. He chose the field of rehabilitation because it is less confining than other branches of medicine and did not require lecturing in front of a group. For thirty-one years Howard Liebgold had struggled with severe claustrophobia.

Until his third year of college, Howard had been confident of his abilities. "I'd always overcome fears. I did sports, I played football. Before the panic attacks came, I always seemed to be able to handle trouble; I never thought of myself as noncourageous. Then one afternoon, sitting in my Shakespeare class, I became unbearably agitated. I couldn't put it into words, but I knew I had to get out of the room. From that moment on, I could not go into any situation that felt confining without feeling extreme dread. My phobia was devastating to my self-image."

As the years passed, Howard coped without divulging the truth even to his wife and children. He was an expert at making plausible excuses to get out of situations that made him nervous. When his sister wanted to get theater tickets, he'd insist, "Don't spend the money. I don't want to see a show. I'm here to see you." He was fine if he drove a car, but could not face the constraint of being a passenger. He was a wonderful parent and spent many hours playing with his children outdoors. He was entertaining and engaging in social situations, as long as he didn't feel closed in. He didn't dance for fear that he would feel trapped with a partner. Just the thought of being restrained made him want to run out of the room.

Howard realized that he couldn't really enjoy anything, not even his long-awaited graduation from medical school, because he was always anticipating fear. "Where will I be sitting?" he worried. "Where will I be standing? What is going to happen if I have to leave?" No one else was aware of his problem except on those embarrassing occasions when the theater tickets turned out to be in the middle of a row and he had to escape. Once when he and his wife were going to a party with another couple, the other man was so insistent about driving that Howard couldn't talk his way out of sitting in the back seat. He had a severe panic attack and had to get out of the car and go back to his own vehicle.

Where he most zealously guarded his secret was in his professional life. "From that first attack on, I never again went into a room without experiencing anxiety. Can you understand what that means for a third-year premed student, who was going to have to attend medical school, then continue on to an internship and one day be confined in operating rooms, delivering babies and attending surgery? My entire life was dedicated to not letting anybody find out because I thought that if anyone did, I wouldn't be able to become a doctor." Once in medical school, Howard broke off relations with a good friend who chose psychiatry: "I was afraid that he would be able to look in my eyes and find out my secret."

Driven by his motivation and commitment, Howard was able to become a doctor. As he put it, "Most of the time I was fighting to stay in a situation." He realized he was phobic and kept his eyes open for any new miracle drug that could solve his problem.

Having fewer choices than are available today, he occasionally took a tranquilizer to reduce his anxiety for a few hours. For a short period he sought relief from anticipatory anxiety with alcohol, but recognized quickly that this could lead to a serious addiction. He never discussed his progressing phobias with his professional associates. At one point he found an independent psychiatrist and went into psychoanalysis for nine months. "I went outside the hospital where I was working because I didn't want anyone there to see me going to the psychiatry department. For me to spend seventeen grand going to another hospital when I didn't have to was significant, but I was desperately concerned about what would happen if people found out I was phobic." His therapy gave him a chance to look at some inner issues, but it didn't help his phobias. Three months after terminating treatment, his psychoanalyst was killed in a traffic accident. "Ironically, the first thing I thought of was that my secret was still safe."

Howard believed that his reputation as a physician dictated what he was allowed to feel. The stereotype that a physician is always strong and does not show vulnerablility made it even more difficult for him to accept his fear. "Sometimes I actually felt like I was the worst physician on Earth and that everybody here was a better doctor than I was because of my phobias. I knew intellectually that wasn't true. I was chief of the largest rehabilitation center in northern California, I was voted California Physician of the Year, and I was compassionate, sympathetic, and smart. But I was scared, and scared was not an acceptable feeling to me."

Howard's story illustrates how self-judgment and concerns about what other people think can trap us even more than our physical limitations. When we define ourselves by our problems, we often obscure our own strengths and abilities. No matter what your lifestyle or profession, you probably have ideas of the image you must maintain so that other people will value you. While having role models and goals can be helpful, if you compare yourself to idealized images and don't allow yourself to be a real human being, you put additional pressure on yourself.

Introducing Bonnie: Fear of Rejection

Bonnie is quiet and thoughtful. She prefers to spend her limited spare time reading or gardening. Remarried ten years ago, her main occupation is keeping up with her two-year-old daughter. Her decision to spend this period of her life as a full-time parent is not based on a need to retreat inside her home. In fact, she is now free of panic and finally relaxed and confident enough to enjoy herself whether at home, on the highway, or at the zoo.

Bonnie's first panic attack occurred after she was divorced and working to support her first child. While driving home from work one evening, she had a sense of unreality and strange visual distortions—the cars in her rearview mirror seemed either too far away or out of proportion. After that experience, she drove only when she absolutely had to, bracing herself and staring straight ahead or distracting herself from her indefinable fear by adding up the numbers on license plates.

Over the years her panic appeared and receded intermittently, surfacing in different situations. Bonnie vividly recalls the discrepancy between what she felt inside and what she let other people see. "I didn't tell anyone what was happening. I was afraid I was going crazy, and just figured I'd better hang on real tight."

Fear of heights became her most debilitating anxiety. "When I got around the windows on the fifth floor of the building where I worked, I felt like they were drawing me toward them and if I wasn't careful I'd be compelled to jump." Many years after she had left her job there, she got that same intense urge on a ski lift. "My heart beat violently, and I had the feeling that I might not be able to stop myself. I didn't jump, but I felt very shaken and didn't dare tell anyone."

That started a period of about two years of panic attacks that increased in frequency and severity. Bonnie was working on a degree in political science. "I had to change some of my courses so I wouldn't have to take classes that were in tall buildings. I was very motivated to stay in school, and forced myself to go back into the classroom the next day if I left early. But all the time, what was going on inside me was just awful."

By then Bonnie was remarried, but she couldn't even tell her husband about her panic attacks. "I didn't know what it was. I couldn't tell anybody. I was afraid of being labeled crazy and being committed. I was afraid of having people reject or abandon me. Other people thought I was calm and collected. I followed the model I learned from my dad, that there is a right way and wrong way to do things. I was a perfectionist and made things look so right."

Like many of us who are prone to panic, Bonnie was a genuinely competent person who often felt knotted up inside while appearing calm and in control. But anxiety grows when fears are kept hidden, especially if they become linked to feelings of self-blame and shame. Although Bonnie coped in the only way she knew, her isolation and fear of rejection added to her anxiety, and she worried that she couldn't keep up her front much longer.

Introducing Edward:
Seeking Relief with Alcohol

Edward works in the personnel division of a large city-government office. His body looks active and projects a strong physical presence even before he speaks. He talks slowly and deliberately, giving a sense that he is choosing his words carefully. He divides his time between his career and his family, doting on his two adopted daughters.

Edward's panic started when he was a high school student. On a field trip to a wind tunnel at a nearby air force base, he became paralyzed with fear while standing on a catwalk a hundred feet above the ground. His fellow students had to hoist him under the arms and carry him down. "They took me into the men's room

and splashed cold water on my face, and I still had butterflies in my stomach for about half an hour afterward.
That incident never totally left me. Sometimes I would
think to myself, 'You might freeze on this one'—but I
never did." Several years passed before Edward had
another incident, this time while driving his car. He
shudders when he remembers the sensation. "I felt like
instead of being flat on the ground, I was flat on the
ceiling, that I was going to fall up."

By his early twenties, Edward was beginning to
have a consistent dread of driving. The area in which he
could navigate kept getting smaller and smaller. He
managed to cover his limitations by tailoring his life to
accommodate his fears. He got a master's degree in
communications and took a job in the personnel department of his university, declining other positions that
would have required him to commute. He managed to
live his life almost entirely within a two-mile radius of
his home. "I didn't have to drive far to work. Although I
was extremely successful at school, if I had gone out in
the real world or gone to graduate school elsewhere, I
would have had to deal with the phobia. In 1978 I interviewed for a position as junior vice president of human
resources at a company about twenty miles away. I
wound up not taking the job because I knew I couldn't
handle the commute. With my friends I was making
excuses for not driving places: I was a good ecologist. I
was a good car pooler. I was on the cutting edge of mass
transit and it was such a neat thing to do. The truth is I
couldn't get in the car and drive the four miles from my
house to the highway."

Edward felt that he had always performed well and convinced himself that he could have a good life by covering up the phobia. Sometimes he got caught in his own deception, for example when he agreed to go somewhere and at the last minute discovered that he just couldn't face the drive. In his late twenties he started dating Ann. "One time she invited me over to her house to have pizza and beer. I got about ten blocks and turned around and went home. I just got too tense. There were lots of times I wouldn't tell her what had really happened; I would lie to her and say someone came by and I couldn't leave."

Edward's anxiety kept getting worse. "I had a full-blown panic attack while driving the shortcut home, so I pulled over to the side of the road. I was miserable. I drove about seven miles an hour hugging the curb and when I came to a parked car, I stopped, held my breath and then practically scraped paint off the side of my car to get around it and close to the curb again."

Edward discovered that alcohol could anesthetize his anxiety for brief periods, sometimes just long enough to drive from one place to another. He didn't have any interest in drinking for pleasure or recreation. He used it purely as a medication to alleviate his anxiety. Eventually, he stopped going anywhere without a handy supply of alcohol.

"I wasn't drinking daily, but I kept three vodka miniatures in the glove compartment. The logic behind the miniatures was that they were small. I could drink them and toss them without littering too badly. If a cop stopped me, I wouldn't have an open container. I chose vodka because it was the purest product—no aldehydes like in scotch or resins like gin. I fooled myself by thinking I was being very rational and health-conscious."

At first Edward thought that what he was doing was a careful, well-thought-out plan. "I was becoming dependent on alcohol but did not consider myself an alcoholic; I was rarely clinically intoxicated." He still had his own definition of alcoholism: "I'll know I am an alcoholic when I pee in my pants. Then I'll know it's gotten out of control and I'll stop. Well, I never peed in my pants. What stopped me was the day my mother came to visit, and I shoved her because I was drunk. In the long run, the alcohol irritated my nervous system even more and began to affect my behavior in other ways."

Panic or anxiety is sometimes the real issue underlying a dependency on alcohol. Many people start to drink in social situations to cover up their discomfort. Alcohol is a depressant and initially relaxes or at least numbs the nervous system. But when it wears off, the anxiety returns. With continued use, alcohol actually makes the nerves more sensitive and less able to tolerate stress. What may seem to give momentary relief delays finding a real solution to the problem.

Introducing Kathy: Prisoner in Her Own Home

Kathy is a capable and intelligent woman. When she talks, her intense brown eyes focus directly on you while her hands move in excited, expressive gestures.

When I went to interview her for the first time in her home, I was drawn to her active hands—lighting a cigarette, petting her dog, or pointing out something she had made. Energetic and motivated, she has used her practical skills to tackle household improvements, sew clothing, and to produce craft items. When Kathy was in her mid thirties, she began to have frequent, unpredictable panic attacks. At one point they became so frightening that she felt she could not leave her house even to go into the front yard.

In the year leading up to this crisis, several things occurred that added stress to Kathy's life. First, her husband's new work shift added strain to their relationship. His expectations that she be home to prepare a full-course dinner in the middle of the afternoon conflicted with Kathy's part-time job and her desire for greater independence. Then her mother became sick and nearly died. Her mother's condition brought up a deep fear of loss, intensified by Kathy's memory of her father's sudden death when she was fourteen.

Kathy carried on with her regular routine and coped with these stresses as well as she could, but strange symptoms began to disturb her. One night while at a carnival with her daughter, she felt as though she was swaying as she walked. The sensation was disturbing, but she assumed it was because of the lights from the rides. A few weeks later when she got upset about something at work, her chest got very tight and she had difficulty breathing. She grabbed a stick of gum and concentrated on chewing it until she felt normal again. She didn't mention these episodes to anyone, but as they started happening more frequently, she became horrified. "It was so irrational. I was fine, and all of a sudden this overwhelming fear took over my whole body. I just felt like I was going to scream. I didn't know what was happening, or why. Nothing was wrong, yet I couldn't get myself under control."

Over the next two years, the episodes occured more frequently. Although increasingly uneasy about going out, Kathy continued to manage her regular routine for several more months. Then one day while standing in a supermarket checkout line, she felt very agitated. "All of a sudden I got this horrid hot flash. It was like fire all over my whole body. I took my coat off and it didn't help." By the time she got her grocery total, she was shaking so badly that she could barely sign her check. "I was thinking, 'I'm going to pass out. What will happen next? What if someone sees me?'"

Although her knees were trembling, she managed to get her groceries to the car and drive home. But when she got back to her house she was shaky and cold. She lay on the couch while her husband and daughter unloaded the groceries. After that she didn't dare leave her house. She stopped working—in fact, she felt as though she almost stopped living—for fear that she would be caught somewhere, alone or in public, and unable to function.

Kathy's behavior was an attempt to prevent frightening feelings by consistently staying away from the situations in which they had occurred. This coping strategy may give immediate relief, but in the long run it reinforces the illusion that neutral situations in your environment are potential threats. Though she knew intellectually that these same conditions had once left her undisturbed, Kathy felt that the carnival lights, the store, even the people walking down the street were causing her panic. She could not stop the automatic reaction of her body at even the thought of going out in public. She described the next year and a half as "watching my life go on about me, without me. I'm living in this house, watching my family do everything they do, and I can't participate in it. They go to work every day, they go to school. Whatever comes into the house, I'm a part of; whatever goes out of the house, I'm not a part of." Kathy became a prisoner in her own home.

Introducing Brian: What Good Is Talking About It?

Brian is tall and slender, the warmth of his eyes a contrast to his otherwise serious expression. He shares a plant-filled flat with his partner Jim and a furry dog that they rescued from the pound. Brian works in the marketing division of a popular sportswear manufacturer. He gets very animated when he talks about his experience, although he admits that just a year ago he would have been too distraught and too ashamed to tell his story to anyone.

Brian's first panic attack occured while flying to Texas. It shook his self-confidence to the core. The son of a commercial pilot, he had flown in airplanes since he was a tiny child. "I had no anticipation of a problem when I got on the plane, but the minute I heard the cabin door slam, I was overwhelmed with the feeling that I had to escape. I sat there dying. I put a magazine in front of my face and tried to read the words, and for brief moments the terror would subside. I really did not know what was going on."

Sitting frozen for the three-hour flight, Brian's body became so tense that all his muscles and joints ached for days afterward. But he had no words to describe his strange feelings, and he didn't tell anyone. "What good is talking about it? I was always told that talk is cheap."

After that incident, his panic spread to other areas—riding on the subway or in someone's car. His digestive system was often in distress, so he sought help for his physical symptoms, finding it easier to describe tangible pain than to discuss irrational feelings. Specialists sent him for numerous tests, including upper and lower gastrointestinal (GI) exams, but they could find nothing wrong with him. Brian got some temporary relief from his stomach pain by going to an acupuncturist. Then he had an episode at work during which he felt an overwhelming sense of losing control; he couldn't even focus his eyes. He became deeply depressed, losing all sense of himself and feeling unable to relate to the things that once brought him joy or pleasure. He took a week off from work and stayed home. He felt as though he would never stop crying.

Panic and phobias can lead to depression when people who are accustomed to performing well find themselves increasingly unable to do things they previously took for granted. Coping by making excuses for not doing things is painful and emotionally debilitating. It not only creates distance between you and others, but it can cut you off from aspects of yourself. When you constantly hear yourself saying, "I'm too tired . . . I'm not interested . . . I don't have any time off to go away . . . ," some part of you starts to believe it. Denying what is important to you can flatten your interest in life and contribute to feelings of depression and isolation from others.

As hard as it is to deal with the actual symptoms of panic, the emotional isolation that comes from not knowing where to turn for help or how to share your experience often causes worse pain than the actual physical symptoms. Discouraged by immediate problems, you may find it hard to maintain a realistic perspective on the future.

You're On Your Way

According to the director of the anxiety and mood disorders clinic at a major California hospital, "Most patients have usually gone to five or six doctors before they come to see me or have an awareness that they might have a psychiatric medical condition such as panic disorder, or panic with agoraphobia. Often by then they have had up to eight special medical tests, including upper GIs, stomach X rays, coronary angiograms, and more. Until the last five to ten years, these anxiety conditions were not well recognized and we didn't have many good treatments. It was not uncommon for physicians to do their best to find physical causes and then tell patients, 'Nothing is wrong; this is just in your head, maybe nerves.'"

Today the health care community is more aware of the occurrence of panic-related conditions, especially in a person who comes in with sudden bursts of extreme anxiety, symptoms that mimic heart attacks or asthma, or digestive disorders that may be related to anxiety. This makes it especially important to give a good detailed medical history, accurately describing the onset and context of symptoms. It's a lot easier to work with a panic disorder or phobia than to cope with the unknown, imagining you have some incurable or indefinable flaw.

Whatever you have done up to now to cope with your fear is the best that you could do, given what you knew. You are not immature, crazy, or wrong. You are a worthwhile human being who has a stress-related disorder that can be alleviated with the proper information and learning skills. When you find the words to communicate your experience, you are on your way to getting the help you need.

How About You?

1. How Have You Coped with Your Fear?

In this chapter you have seen some of the ways people have coped with their fear. Edward used alcohol to calm himself and worked within a two-mile radius of his home; Howard made excuses and chose a specialty that would not require being confined. In your journal, make a list of the things you do to cope with anxiety— not just in times of major crisis, but in response to everyday emotional stresses as well.

Here are some examples: Do you avoid uncomfortable situations? Do you make up excuses? Do you hide your feelings? Do you focus on the needs of others so they won't know how uncomfortable or inadequate you feel?

Situation	How I Cope
Invitation to a party	Give an excuse; say I have work to do
1.	_____
2.	_____

Look over your list and notice how your methods of coping affect you. What aspects of your behavior support you? What coping strategies exhaust you or make you feel more alone?

2. Telling Yourself the Truth

In your journal, write down the excuses you give to other people—and especially to yourself—when your fear prevents some activity. Then ask yourself what you would say if you spoke frankly, in spite of your discomfort. Write your inner truth in your journal. Remember, this exercise is not to be used to judge or blame yourself, but is a tool to understand yourself better.

1. <u>Yes, I *do* want to come to your birthday dinner, but I'm concerned about meeting so many new people. If I come, I may only stay a short time.</u>

2. _____

Identify Your Feelings

Does telling the truth to yourself bring up any feelings? Notice whether acknowledging your feelings helps you become more clear about what is bothering you and what you want. Record your observations. For example:

1. <u>I'm *angry* at Joe for driving so fast when I'm in the car with him. I want him to consider my feelings and desires.</u>

2. _____

3. _____

Suppressing your true feelings depletes your energy. Telling the truth to yourself and facing your feelings reminds you of what is important to you and is a necessary step toward being motivated to take charge of your life.

3. Looking at Your Role: Self-Expectations

What do you expect of yourself? In your journal, make two columns. Head the first column "My Roles," and the second column "Qualities." Now, in capital letters, write your various roles in the first column—for example, DEPARTMENT SUPERVISOR, PARENT, BIG BROTHER, OLDEST DAUGHTER, BEST FRIEND, and so on. List all qualities that you think you should have for each role.

My Roles	Qualities
BEST FRIEND	always listen, don't disappoint, come to birthday party, don't disagree
1.	_____
2.	_____

Read over what you have written. What do you demand of yourself? How do you feel when you can't meet your own expectations? What do you say to yourself when you fall short? In your journal, write your observations.

3

The Turning Point

For many people who suffer from panic, the turning point comes when they identify what is going on and have a name for it. This does not mean that they have found a magic cure or an instant solution. Time and practice are needed to reverse patterns that have become habitual. But a big shift occurs when you move from feeling completely powerless and frightened by your situation to understanding what is happening and realizing that there is something you can do to change it. Having the words to describe your condition can give you a bridge to rebuild relationships to friends and family. The energy that once was used to guard your secret can now be directed toward healing.

Getting Started

After my brother gave me the phone number of the therapist he'd heard about, I called her right away. In our first meeting, I felt like a child who had finally found someone to answer her questions. Hilda knew what I was talking about. Nothing I said shocked her. Five years of pent-up frustration poured out of me. Listening to my story, she nodded her head in understanding. Yes, yes, yes. All the sensations I described were classic symptoms of panic attacks. Although they were awful to experience, she assured me that these attacks would not kill me and would not cause heart attacks or lead to insanity. Furthermore, these symptoms could not be sustained at such a high level indefinitely. They would reach a peak and then gradually subside unless I refueled my anxiety with more fearful thoughts.

Most important of all, Hilda told me that I could change. She assured me that I would be able to approach difficult situations in small increments, setting my own pace and using skills that had helped millions of people. As she heard me sigh with relief, she added, "This is not such a big tragedy. Lots of people have it and get better. Let's start by looking at what's going on."

Hilda helped me see how my initial panic attack had developed into a phobia. *Of course* I had started to avoid the situation in which it occurred. *Of course* I had grown afraid of my lack of control over my mind and body. Without an understanding of what was happening and without skills to manage it, I couldn't risk getting caught in a situation where I might feel totally helpless. At the end of the session, Hilda suggested we start with breathing and relaxation exercises. She assured me that when I was ready, she would go driving with me. For the first time in years, I had a little bit of hope that I wouldn't have to continue living as I had been. There were things I could do to help myself.

This Is Curable

Howard still gets tears in his eyes when he tells the story of the first time he heard there were tools that could stop his panic and cure his claustrophobia. It was 1984, the year the Olympics were being held in Los Angeles. "My son wanted to go to the Olympic Games. Every day I read newspaper articles about two million people turning the L.A. freeways into parking lots. I thought, 'No way in the world could I do that.' But I read an article that said the chance of getting tickets to the opening games was only one in forty-five hundred. My son didn't know I was phobic and I thought, 'One in forty-five hundred? I'll send in my application and tell him that we're probably not going to get the tickets.'"

Nine months before the Olympics began, Howard received a letter saying that he had been awarded two tickets to the opening games. Unable to stop his mind from racing ahead to what might happen nine months in the future, he had a panic attack while reading the letter. The next day he got subpoenas in the mail for a big lawsuit in which he was treating the injured party. Courts were another place where he felt phobic, and he dreaded having to testify. Within twenty-four hours he had two terrifying situations to contend with.

"That night an incredible thing happened. I saw an item on the evening news about somebody who couldn't

drive across bridges and was working with a local group
that helped people with phobias. The next morning
there was a related article in the paper about the same
group. I called the director and had an interview with
her. The memory still brings me to tears. She was the
first person who said that what I had was curable. I had
never heard that word before."

Howard decided that "whatever the hell had to be
done," he would do it. He enrolled in the group program. "The most important part was using the tools
they gave me. If you did your deep breathing and your
logical thinking, you could turn off that panic response.
It never was under my control before. The first thing I
realized was that if I could control panic, that would
change my world."

Howard did every practice exercise and homework
assignment as diligently as he had studied in medical
school. "One of the assignments was to tell people you
had a phobia. Although I talked to my family when I
started the program, I didn't tell my colleagues at first.
I couldn't get the word *phobia* out, so I told them that
I was taking a class on assertiveness. A few weeks later I
did tell my professional associates that I was attending a
class on phobias because I was claustrophobic."
Howard laughs, "Nobody seemed to faint or drop
dead." Howard also called his friend who had chosen
psychiatry and let him know why he had cut off their
friendship while in medical school.

Within four weeks Howard saw an enormous
change. "I had an emotional breakthrough one night. I
was sitting in a movie theater watching *The Natural*,

and tears were running down my cheeks because I was in the middle of a row. I had never been in that seat before without anxiety. I knew I had my life back."

Although it took another year before Howard could do everything that had previously intimidated him, he immediately made a commitment to dedicate part of his life to helping other people with panic and phobias. "I wrote an article for the hospital newspaper, so two million people knew that I was phobic. I got a raise, which I thought was kind of funny because I always had this great fear of what would happen if people found out." Howard knew he didn't have the time to provide very much individual attention, so he went to Canada to research a large-scale self-help program called Secure. He got permission to use some of their material and techniques and, with the collaboration of the health education department of the hospital where he worked, he set up a ten-week class for curing phobias and shyness. He called his class Phobease.

Each Step Leads to the Next

After Bonnie finished her political science degree, she decided to work on a research project at home. During that period her panic attacks and her phobic thinking had escalated to the point that she didn't feel safe even in her own kitchen. One afternoon she heard an airplane overhead and began to get anxious, thinking it could crash into her house. That's when she realized she had to seek professional help.

Although it took some effort to find the information and tools she needed, each step she took brought her closer to a solution. First she called a counselor she knew and got a referral to a psychologist. Over the course of a year's therapy, Bonnie began to explore her feelings and look at some important influences from her childhood. She recognized that she had never questioned the family attitudes that made her so rigid. She also realized that she had never resolved feelings related to her mother's death. "My mother got cancer, was hospitalized and died when I was nine years old. We didn't go to the funeral, and my dad withdrew emotionally. My stepmother later told me that as kids we were always playing funeral. I think the loss of my mother played a key role in not telling anyone about my feelings. I was afraid that if I told them what was going on inside, they would leave me."

The counseling sessions gave Bonnie some insight into how she was coping, but did not specifically address her panic attacks. Sometimes she had a panic attack right in the counselor's office but was too embarrassed to say anything. Bonnie told me, "My psychologist didn't know what I was experiencing, and for a long time I didn't know she didn't know!"

Although Bonnie decided to discontinue her therapy, it had pointed her in an important direction. She knew that her problem had to do with anxiety. An inveterate researcher, she went to the school library and read every book she could find on the subject. She figured out that she was having panic attacks and that she was agoraphobic. She felt relieved because for the first time she understood what was happening to her. Despite her fears of rejection, her new understanding gave her the courage to talk to her husband about her condition.

"It took several more months before I was ready to tell him. I did it only because the message I got from all the books was that to heal from panic and phobia, a person needs to *deal with the feelings of shame* that come from thinking that there is something terribly wrong with you. The road is easier and quicker if you have the support of those around you. We had already been married for eight years, the last few of which were really hard for me. I finally became convinced that I should take a big risk and tell my husband. I had been so effective at disguising my pain that he was genuinely surprised to hear about my struggle with fear. He was very willing to support me in any way he could."

Bonnie is self-motivated and learns best with a self-help approach, so she did further research and found a home-study course with weekly lessons on cassettes. She felt comfortable getting instruction from tapes she could listen to at home and repeat as often as she needed. She liked working at her own pace.

"In the beginning I had more of a hope than a conviction that I would get better. I did the program on faith. It said to practice my relaxation exercise twenty times a day—ten times with the tape and ten times without the tape—going mentally through my body and relaxing it. I did it as often as I could. It took about eight weeks before I felt any change in myself. Then I noticed for longer periods of the day, I didn't feel high anxiety. I started to have times when I felt like my old normal self."

Healing Body and Spirit

After Edward had been drinking for about two years, his nerves became so ragged that it was hard to drive even the two miles to work. One of the problems with using alcohol to relieve anxiety is that the body builds a tolerance to alcohol and it takes larger and larger amounts to have an effect. Not only was Edward physically affected, his self-esteem was at the lowest point ever. He made a decision to go to Alcoholics Anonymous. "I knew I needed specific skills to face my phobias, but I first had to stop drinking. The honesty and compassion of the people in the fellowship of A.A. gave me a solid foundation for staying sober." Once Edward felt more secure in his own sobriety, he began to look for a phobia treatment program. TERRAP, an acronym for Territorial Apprehension, was one of the first panic and phobia treatment programs to combine therapy, education, and behavior modification skills. Edward located a group right on the campus where he was working, run by the founder of the program, Dr. Arthur Hardy.

For Edward, TERRAP and A.A. together formed a complete recovery program. "I needed the specific suggestions and practical guidance I got in the phobia treatment group, but it didn't really do anything for my spiritual needs. From A.A. I got the spiritual support that helped me get over my feelings of shame and inadequacy."

Edward realized that his healing process could not be separate from his life. He showed a pamphlet describing phobic fears to his girlfriend, Ann. This was his way of opening a discussion on the subject and inviting her to participate in the phobia treatment program. Ann and Edward learned more about each other and developed mutual trust by making this program a part of their relationship. Soon after the class was over, they decided to get married.

Rebuilding a Bridge to Others

One day, while reading *Consumer Reports*, Brian noticed an ad for a booklet on coping with anxiety. "I didn't know what anxiety was. I had never put a handle on what was wrong with me, but something told me to order this booklet. I had almost forgotten about it when it arrived three weeks later. It gave a list of symptoms, most of which I had, and a lot of which I'd never had. But that was the first time I had a name to call what was going on with me."

Having a name for his traumatic episodes helped Brian put his situation in perspective. "I found a new doctor within walking distance of my house and laid it on the table." When Brian described his symptoms, the doctor agreed that it sounded like panic disorder and referred him to a psychiatrist. He also sent Brian to a brain specialist to rule out any organic cause for his occasional difficulty focusing his eyes. The psychiatrist started him on a low dose of an antidepressant medication. Originally developed for mood disorders, the antidepressant family of drugs has been shown to be effective in reducing the panic response.

But the biggest changes in Brian's life came from talking to other people about his situation. He found out that his boss had panic attacks too, and one of Brian's coworkers admitted he had moved closer to the office to avoid riding the train to work. Brian told his friends that he was looking for help, and soon got the name of a private therapist who worked specifically with phobias. This therapist taught him techniques and skills to help him relax and begin the recovery process. As he renewed trust in himself, Brian also began to feel more comfortable socializing again. I first met him a month after he started individual therapy. He was parking his car in front of his house when I arrived. Looking very satisfied with himself, he told me, "I drove myself today . . . like a big boy."

Finding Someone Who Cares

Although she felt very uncomfortable leaving her house, Kathy was able to go with her husband to keep an apppointment with a psychiatrist. He wrote her a prescription for medication, but she had heard some controversial reports about the drug and didn't want to use it. He didn't offer her any other alternative, and she felt that her life was at a dead end. Then a relative told her about a news article describing the weekly class on phobias taught by Howard Liebgold.

"In the past I had felt very intimidated by doctors, but when I called the hospital, Dr. Liebgold took my call personally. He listened to my story and assured me I wasn't crazy. I started to cry on the phone because I felt like he cared about me. He said I didn't have to dig up my past; I didn't have to take the medication if I preferred not to; I could start right now by learning how to control my responses. For me, he was an angel from heaven, someone who understood what I was going through."

Since Kathy could not come to the class, Dr. Liebgold agreed to work with her by phone. She ordered his workbook and completed the weekly reading and assignments, calling him every Friday to report on her progress and get additional guidance. Encouraged by his confidence in her, Kathy began to trust that her panic, though very frightening, would not get any worse.

Remembering his own years of suffering alone, Liebgold encouraged Kathy to reach out to others. "Stop closing the door and using all your energy to keep it shut. You need to let it out and tell someone." Instead of making up an excuse for not working at the graduation-night event at her daughter's school, she told the truth to Trina, another parent. She found out that she could participate in other ways, by making phone calls and doing some planning. "That was good. It was like therapy for me because I could talk to people in the outside world and participate in the event in my own way."

She also learned that Trina had suffered from agoraphobia ten years earlier. "When Trina and I talked, I found out she had the same feelings I did. It meant everything to me, to be assured that I was a normal person and could get over this, by someone who knew what she was talking about." That was the beginning of a close friendship between the two women. Their bond became an ongoing source of encouragement for Kathy.

We're All in This Together

I was at home one afternoon when I got a call from a friend. "Quick, turn on the radio," he said. "There's a program on about panic attacks." I turned to the sports station and heard Earl Campbell—ex-football star of the Houston Oilers and MVP (most valuable player) three years in a row. He was talking about the time he stopped at a red light and his chest started beating like a bass drum. He thought he was having a heart attack. Earl saw seven doctors and even had a coronary angiogram before he got the correct diagnosis of panic disorder.

I went to hear Earl speak that night at the local high school. He was totally unlike the stereotype of a frightened person. His manner was calm and personal, his appearance the epitome of strength. He was touring the country to educate people about panic by telling his own story. Four years earlier, panic had so taken over his life that he couldn't go out to run the four-mile course around his neighborhood, a workout he had done regularly for many years. He told us that in his community in Texas, every house has a different color mailbox in front of it. As part of his recovery process, he ran one mailbox farther each day until he could run the whole circuit back to his home. The audience in the packed auditorium was encouraged to hear how both medication and behavioral therapy were helping him.

Talking about your situation doesn't help only you. When you disclose what is true for you, it gives other people the courage to share their own experience. Almost every time I mention my phobia in a social situation or at a presentation, someone comes up to me afterward and says, "I have that too," or, "I didn't realize until I heard you speak that my dread of going to school is related to your trouble driving." As we bring our experiences into the open, we start reducing the barriers between ourselves and others.

It is natural to feel vulnerable when you first start talking about your condition. Use good judgment in choosing someone to confide in. Start with someone who is genuinely interested in you and will listen with compassion. You don't have to tell your whole story; the point is to take the secret out of it. You can simply say that you have a condition in which too much adrenalin causes you to have panic attacks. You can add that you are learning some stress-reduction skills to work on the problem. When you express your own feelings and doubts, you often find out how much you have in common with other people. Like Brian and Kathy, you may even discover that others in your circle of friends and associates can identify with what you are saying and are eager to share their experiences with you. You are not the only one with these feelings.

Turn It Around

Until I spoke to Hilda, my therapist, I really did think that I had made up this problem and should be able to just drop it. But I couldn't drop it. I needed information and tools to turn it around. I say "turn it around" because *a phobia can become a progressive disorder* that reinforces itself. The more you withdraw, the more likely you are to be afraid of the same thing next time or to avoid a new situation that appears threatening. Each time you hesitate, you undermine your sense of mastery.

The good news is that the reverse is also true. Healing is also progressive. Every time you feel an improvement, you reinforce your sense of confidence in yourself and in your power to change. Taking action toward your recovery is really making a complete turn. There are different ways of learning and many paths to getting better. Even when you don't have all the answers, you can take an active role by getting more information, listening to your intuition, and setting your priorities.

Whatever stage you are in, there is a step you can take. If you are in the early stages of developing avoidance patterns or just discovering that you have phobias, you may want to do more reading, talk to your doctor, or seek professional consultation. Perhaps you have already identified your problem but have become discouraged with your progress. Your next step may be to make a renewed commitment to using your tools to create a stronger support system. You may not always get all the answers you need immediately, but each time you reach out instead of giving up, you are moving toward freedom. Your intention to get better and your perseverance will lead you to the right sources of help.

How About You?

1. Telling Other People

Break the ice by telling another person about your experience. Once you say it, you'll find that you no longer have to exhaust your energy to keep your secret. In your journal, make a list of the people you think would understand. Look over your list and choose the best candidate. Use good judgment and choose a person who is important to you and whom you can trust. Set aside a time to talk together or write a simple letter. It's usually easier to *keep the discussion simple.* Your task is to get the facts out, not to dig up the roots of the problem. If your friend wants more information, you can always elaborate.

2. Planning Your Next Step

There is a Chinese saying, "A journey of a thousand miles must begin with a single step." What is the step that can begin your journey? In your journal, write some ideas of what your next step might be. It can be a simple step: for instance, finishing this book. Or you may decide to talk to a friend, as in the previous exercise. Maybe you need to get more information from the library, your doctor or health care advisor, or a therapist? There are some helpful resources listed in the back of the book starting on page 279.

Section II

Techniques and Tools

TOOLS

I don't trust
this calm
'cause there's always
"what if" and
"remember last time . . . ,"

But wait,

'cause if I ever felt
"that way" again
I'd take my tools
and build safeness.

I don't need to trust
or distrust the calm
'cause I'm the builder
who always wears
her tool belt.

—Dale K.S. Ireland

4

Designing Your Own Program for Healing

Educating yourself about panic and phobias and researching treatment options are an integral part of taking charge of your life again. Don't be intimidated by the word *treatment*. Getting treatment means obtaining the skills needed to change your fear response. In most cases, this response is a learned behavior that can be unlearned. If you've ever participated in a sport, you know that habits, such as holding your tennis racquet a certain way or bending your arm when it should be straight, take some time and effort to change. New behavior may feel awkward at first. Yet, with the right instruction and consistent practice, you can improve your game. Recovering from phobias is like that too. Although a phobia class or treatment program may be brief—usually a minimum of two to four months—the job of practicing the skills and keeping active in newly regained territory may last years or even a lifetime.

Before deciding on a treatment plan it is always wise to talk with your doctor or health practitioner to rule out any medical conditions whose symptoms resemble those associated with panic. When you do seek treatment, describe your entire behavior pattern and its history to assist your practitioner in making an accurate diagnosis. Keeping a record of your symptoms and fear-triggers will provide valuable information to help describe your condition. Play an active role in your treatment by asking questions, evaluating what is helping and what is not, and putting into practice the things you learn.

The Building Blocks of Successful Treatment

An effective learning program usually includes four basic components, which may be supplemented by medication if you and your health care practitioner decide it is appropriate. They are:

1. *Physical relaxation:* Using breathing and progressive relaxation techniques to release body tension and reduce excessive adrenalin secretion.
2. *Thought changing:* Learning to stop and transform the fearful thoughts that trigger anxiety and set off the body's alarm system.
3. *Desensitization or exposure therapy:* Learning to function successfully in areas you have avoided, by progressing from small steps to larger challenges. As you master each stage using your new skills, you become *desensitized* to the fear stimulus, just as a person with allergies takes progressively larger doses of an allergen until the chemical no longer elicits a physical response.

4. *Life skills:* Developing or reinforcing habits and attitudes that enhance your confidence in managing everyday situations. These include assertiveness and communication skills that help you express, rather than deny, your feelings, desires, and needs.

The components described above are the building blocks of what is called *cognitive-behavioral therapy.* "Cognitive" simply means thinking. In territorial phobias, agoraphobia, and social phobias, cognitive therapy is a technique that helps us discover and change the unrealistic or fear-producing thought patterns that underlie our panic and dread. The behavioral part of the program consists of changing our actions. The most critical task is twofold: first, to replace the fear reaction with a calming response through relaxation; and then, through progressive desensitization, to return to the threatening situation. For many people, having the cognitive-behavioral tools is a tremendous relief. Using their new skills to conquer fear, even in small increments, is a source of motivation and renewed self-confidence.

Going to an Individual Therapist

Over the years of my healing process, I have tried several different approaches. In the beginning I really needed some hand-holding and a chance to talk about the years of hiding and confusion. It was very helpful for me to have the focused, personal attention provided by an individual therapist. Hilda was very practical. From our second session on, we spent more time in my car than we did in her office—so much time, in fact, that I called her my driving therapist. The first time we went out together, she slid casually into the passenger seat. "Hilda," I said, "you're not going to ride in the car while I drive, are you?" "Of course I am," she responded without a moment's hesitation. "I have ridden with hundreds of people with phobias and no one has ever lost control of the car."

When you research professional help, find out if the therapist will see you only in the office, or will also work with you in the situations that have been stressful. Some therapists believe it is more effective for you to do all your fieldwork on your own, while others will accompany you to the supermarket, ride the train with you, or even take a short plane flight with you. It can be very helpful to have someone right there to check out your thoughts and help you learn how to respond differently to the things that trigger your reactions.

Therapists who work primarily in their office can help you determine what additional support you need from friends or family members. This may mean asking a friend or relative to go places with you or to be on call in case you want to talk, be picked up, or need some kind of reassuring contact. No matter how much help you get, however, you have to make a commitment to keep practicing on your own.

Introducing Alicia:
Getting Support from a Group

Alicia is living with her husband in a smaller house now that her daughter has graduated from college and moved to her own apartment. Alicia looks confident and composed, and naturally fits the image of the professional career woman who once did public relations work for a fund-raising foundation. Yet she has great difficulty in any social situation in which she has to make eye contact or casual conversation. Alicia's areas of anxiety are characteristic of what is called *social phobia.* For her, the experience of being in a support group was almost as valuable as the skills she learned there. The fact that everyone else understood what it was like to have "irrational" fears made it possible for her to open up.

As long as Alicia was working she kept her phobia in check. After she decided to take some time off from work, her discomfort and dread began to take over. She became increasingly apprehensive and stopped going out by herself, except to a few places where she felt safe. Her fear of being humiliated in front of others prevented her from attending social events, taking classes, or finding a new job. "It's more than an issue of self-confidence," she told me. "I am confident that I do things well, and in many situations I am a calm person."

Her response to the Chinese students' democracy movement protests in Tiananmen Square in 1989 reveals the intensity of her inner agitation. "What happened there is as close as you can come to how I feel. They took the kids who were protesting, put numbers around their chests, and paraded them in front of everyone. Then they took them out and shot them. For what? For standing up and saying they have a right to be counted as people. That's my fear—that someone's going to single me out for something basically benign, ridicule me in front of the *entire world,* and then take me out and shoot me. Though I know that is not what will really happen, I feel paralyzed by the fear."

Alicia felt she was at a standstill in her life until a chance conversation brought her some new information. Although she often avoided answering the phone, she returned a call to a woman who needed to get an address from her. In the course of the conversation, the woman started talking about her own success in an eighteen-week phobia treatment program. Alicia was encouraged by what she heard and was willing to take a risk that might help her get on with her life. She went to an individual interview and signed up for the group. "The first meeting was the hardest," she admits. "When we were asked to introduce ourselves to each other, I didn't think I could make it through the evening." Alicia soon discovered that she wasn't the only one who was uncomfortable. She also found it very helpful to hear other people talk about things that were hard for them, and she felt less intimidated after listening to their concerns.

I met Alicia for the first time in that phobia group. A camaraderie developed among the twelve of us. Although our phobias took different forms, we had much in common. When we talked about our lives we were amazed to discover that some of the other people had similar childhood experiences. "Our family didn't talk about feelings when our mother died," said one, and another recounted, "My older sister was the one in our family who criticized everything I did."

"I never before ran into anyone who talked about these things," Alicia confided. "I thought all my experiences were unique." As the weeks passed, Alicia became more spontaneous, speaking out and sharing her ideas and feelings. "The group affected me greatly. It gave me back a lot of self-confidence. I could say something and no one would say, 'That's the stupidest thing I ever heard.' They would be enthusiastic, and I could see that the other people might even be able to get something out of what I said."

Participating in a group helped us all see ourselves in a new light. It boosted our self-esteem and confidence to discover how much we really could do, both for ourselves and to support others. One man was uncomfortable eating in restaurants. Several participants met him at a local coffee shop before class so he could practice by being out with them. A woman in the group told me that it had helped her to follow a car driven by a friend. Since I was nervous about driving home in the dark after the meetings, she offered to drive in front of me on the freeway, promising to pull over with me if I flashed my blinker to indicate that I needed to stop. Being with others who were learning the same skills gave us a chance to brag about our successes and receive compassionate understanding about our disappointments. As we got to know each other, it was a welcome relief to find ourselves laughing and relaxing together. We agreed, "There's nothing so terrible about us—we're not such a bad lot!"

In a group situation you have the opportunity to relate to people who share some common issues, and you get a chance to learn from their experiences. For this reason, groups are a very effective forum for phobia treatment, although there are a few things to watch for. You can get lost in a group if you have a hard time asking for attention. In order to get the maximum benefit you have to take the initiative to get the support you need. Another possible pitfall of group work is "symptom swapping"—when you listen to other people's symptoms or problems, you may start to "borrow" them. Whether you participate in a treatment group run by a professional or a peer support group facilitated by other recovering phobics, it is important to find out the guidelines for sharing experiences and to let the group know what works and doesn't work for you. In some groups, participants make an agreement to talk about what is helping instead of dwelling on their symptoms.

Today many different group programs are available, some through organizations that specifically treat panic and anxiety disorders, others sponsored by local hospitals, health centers, or universities. A national organization called Phobics Anonymous promotes peer support groups throughout the country. People who have healed their phobias are often effective in teaching those who are seeking help.

Visiting the Phobease Class

A few months after our first interview, I decided to visit Howard Liebgold's class. I wanted to see how he approached teaching in a room with dozens of people with phobias, some of whom might want to flee at any moment. When I entered the lobby of the hospital where the class was held, a cardboard sign taped next to the elevator jolted me right out of my thoughts.

PHOBEASE CLASS
THIRD-FLOOR CONFERENCE ROOM
STAIRWAY TO THE RIGHT

I immediately understood the significance of the sign. I could remember walking up three, four, even six flights of stairs rather than ride alone in an elevator. I sighed with gratitude for being free of that fear. Feeling a connection to the people waiting upstairs in the classroom, I walked into the elevator and pushed number three.

To my surprise, almost sixty people were already seated around rectangular tables arranged in a horseshoe. They looked like a typical cross-section of people from the Bay Area, some men and women still in their office clothes, others in sweatsuits or blue jeans. I saw people from different ethnic backgrounds and age groups, including an elderly couple, and even several school-age children. Some of the participants had come alone, and others were there with a friend or relative to give them the security of having a familiar person to turn to.

I sat at one of the tables near the back of the room and read the handwritten signs propped randomly on the tables: FACE THE FEAR AND IT WILL DISAPPEAR. COMFORT IS NOT YOUR GOAL, LIVING IS YOUR GOAL. YOU STOP BEING PHOBIC WHEN YOU STOP THINKING PHOBIC.

Dr. Liebgold entered, stopping to clasp a few hands on his way to the front of the room.

On this first night of the ten-week program, Dr. Liebgold gave some basic information about panic and phobias. "The dictionary definition of phobias as irrational bothered me," he told the class. "I was not irrational. I was a responsible physician, head of a rehabilitation center, logical and clear headed, but I was severely phobic." He added that phobics are "highly energetic, warm, compassionate, intelligent, caring, enthusiastic, sensitive, and imaginative people." It was refreshing to hear a doctor speak, not only explaining medical theories, but using his own experiences to dramatize the information as well. The potential for change seems more plausible when you hear the learning tools described by someone who has successfully used them.

Halfway through the class we stopped for a break. I saw Dr. Liebgold walk toward the back of the room. "This is a special evening," he whispered to me as he passed by on his way to greet a woman sitting a few rows behind me. I heard them both laugh and then they gave each other a hug. As Dr. Liebgold walked away, he leaned toward me and confided, "That was a hug worth waiting for."

The woman he had just met was Kathy. For eight months she had called him every Friday, taken his advice, and used the exercises he had recommended. After practicing the tools and techniques you will read about in the next section, she was no longer housebound. Tonight, accompanied by her sister, she had come to the Phobease class for the first time.

Home Study Approaches

If you are not able to get to a location where treatment is offered, or if you prefer to learn on your own, you can begin at home. An increasing number of books, tapes, and home study courses for the layperson are now available. Self-help workbooks provide step-by-step processes and information you can work with on your own. You can also order a home study program on videotape or audiocassettes. Several organizations offer both informational lectures and weekly lessons similar to the series Bonnie used. "The program started with educational information about phobias and what kind of person gets them," she explained. "Then it went on to teach techniques to reduce panic, stop fearful thoughts, change self-defeating attitudes, and go on with your life."

Bonnie found that the fifteen-week self-help cassette program allowed her to reinforce her learning skills and work at her own pace. "I usually listened to each tape several times a week. Written material went along with the tapes. The nice thing about it was I could listen to it no matter what I was doing—cleaning up, doing dishes, even driving the car." Bonnie feels she learns best on her own because with books and tapes she can take the time to digest and integrate new information.

In addition to the practical tools offered in home study materials, they provide some perspective to help you decide if you need professional treatment. Becoming fully informed will take the mystery out of your situation and give you the confidence that comes from being a full participant in your healing.

Medication

While some people prefer to work exclusively with the behavioral skills, others use medication in conjunction with their basic program. Until the 1980s, tranquilizers were the medication most commonly prescribed to anyone suffering symptoms of anxiety. They provided temporary relief but didn't stop or cure panic. Recent advances in psychopharmacology have produced specific antianxiety, antipanic, and antidepressant drugs for treating panic symptoms and lessening anticipatory anxiety. Each medication has some advantages and disadvantages. Some are taken daily and may take several weeks before they are effective. Others can be used on an as-needed basis to lower anxiety in a specific situation. Using medication can be beneficial, especially in conjunction with a learning program.

On the advice of a psychiatrist, Brian took an antidepressant for six months. Although originally designed to alleviate depression, antidepressants have been found to be effective in reducing the panic response. "I didn't like having to take a drug several times a day or the dry mouth it caused," Brian said, "but I had become so unnerved by my experience of panic that I felt unteachable at first." In addition to taking the medication, he found a phobia specialist to teach him the cognitive and behavioral skills he needed. When he discontinued his medication after six months, he had confidence in his ability to rely on the tools he had acquired. If you have become depressed from years of coping, or experience a level of anxiety that prevents you from working on new learning skills, medication may restore your stability enough to work on your healing process.

If you want to consider taking medication, you must discuss your options carefully with a physician, psychopharmacologist, or psychiatrist. You will need to collaborate with a medical professional to monitor the effects and dosages of any drug because the response to any given medication varies from person to person. Find out the exact purpose of the specific drug and the recommended duration of use. Ask about your doctor's experience using it with other patients. Some good questions to ask are: What is the optimal dosage, the long-term benefits, risks, and side effects? If this choice doesn't help or has uncomfortable side effects, are there other alternatives? What is the withdrawal procedure? Is the medication physically or psychologically addictive? Psychological addiction means that although the body can easily adjust to decreased dosages, you may be afraid to stop using the drug if you aren't convinced that you can control your reactions without it. That is one of the reasons why a cognitive-behavioral program is essential.

Several of the people I interviewed were upset that they had been referred to a psychiatrist. They didn't think they needed psychiatric treatment. When football star Earl Campbell told his story on the radio, he said he was surprised when he discovered that the seventh or eighth doctor he was directed to was a psychiatrist. He told the audience, "I was mad because I had to go see a psychiatrist. I didn't want to accept that." But when the doctor handed him a pamphlet on panic disorder, he knew he had come to the right place.

74   *Journey from Anxiety to Freedom*

People who suffer from panic are most often well-adjusted, communicative, and effective in most areas of their lives. But in many cases, a psychiatrist is the professional best equipped to make a diagnosis of panic disorder, or panic disorder with phobias, and to prescribe drugs if indicated. As Brian found out, you may need to do some additional searching to find a phobia therapist or group because few psychiatrists provide instruction or cognitive-behavioral therapy.

You are the one who has to live with the decisions you make, so it is important to take the extra time and effort to ask all the questions you have and make your decision about medication only when you are satisfied with the answers. Your doctor may respond to your discomfort and be eager to give you an immediate solution. But the doctor's main source of information often comes from trial studies conducted by the pharmaceutical companies that produce and market the drugs. You may want to do some research yourself. Several books on anxiety have sections on medication. *The Anxiety and Phobia Workbook* by Edmund Bourne, Ph.D., has a chapter that provides basic information on the use of different antianxiety medications. *Beyond Prozac* by Michael Norden, M.D., describes the use, advantages, and disadvantages of drugs currently available, and also offers non-drug alternatives that have a calming effect on the nervous system. In addition, you can explore the options at your local health food store or vitamin department. Herbal supplements, enzyme formulas, and homeopathic remedies are sometimes very effective for those of us who have sensitive nervous systems.

Medication by itself does not eliminate all anxiety or reverse your behavior patterns. Whether or not you choose to use medication, you will benefit from learning the basic relaxation, thought-changing, and gradual-exposure skills. With these skills you will build confidence in yourself rather than in a drug or another person as your primary source of safety.

Engaging Family and Friends in Your Treatment

Members of your family and your close friends are affected by your fears and often are eager to understand what is going on. They too may feel discouraged or frustrated, and uncertain how to help you. They may also be confused about their own feelings and needs. Some programs welcome a spouse or support person, who may attend with you or meet separately in their own support group. When family members are truly interested and become involved in your healing, they often learn a lot about themselves, even if their initial intention was to help you get better.

Ann attended TERRAP with Edward. When she met with other support people, they discussed the issues and frustrations they faced as partners or family members of the person with phobias. She admitted, "Originally, it was hard for me to understand what

Edward was making such a big deal about. I myself have had panicky feelings, but it never occurred to me to avoid a situation. I really wanted to say, 'Snap out of it and grow up!' Being in the group taught me patience." Ann acknowledged that she learned more about herself and some of her own issues by attending the group. Both Edward and Ann agree that being in the group brought them closer together, helped them build trust, and taught them how to be more supportive of each other.

When Kathy was almost homebound, she relied on her husband to do the things that she couldn't do, such as shopping and errands. But she couldn't count on him to give her emotional support or to accompany her so she could leave the house. "I don't have an easy time asking him to help me with what I need; he is not calm or patient." The person who became her main support was the parent from her daughter's school whom she first talked to about her agoraphobia.

With the compassion that grew out of her own experience with agoraphobia ten years earlier, Trina became both a friend and a coach for Kathy. "She got me started when I couldn't leave my house. She took me to doctors' appointments; she helped me do things one step at a time. Trina encouraged me to think about things I would love to do again: 'Just imagine coming out and seeing your daughter graduate from high school.' She planted the idea in my mind that it was possible. She was always understanding, gently prodding me but never impatient with me."

Each of us must discover how much we can do on our own and to what degree we need professional guidance and help from the people in our lives. Most of the work is up to us: to make a commitment to do the daily work, to practice the relaxation skills until they are as automatic as anxiety once was, to stop scaring ourselves with "fear thoughts," and to muster the courage to challenge our phobias. Yet, no matter how motivated we are, few of us can do this all alone. As human beings we need to talk about our experiences and to have the care and respect of those in our lives. We need some kind of cheering section of people who understand that even a small action, such as going down the street alone or stepping into a store, is a big victory for us. Part of our healing process is to tell others what helps us to help ourselves.

Other Forms of Therapy

Many people find that once they learn the skills to confront their phobias, they want to change other aspects of their lives as well. If your anxiety has been exacerbated by years of repressing your feelings and hiding fears, counseling can help you change attitudes and longtime behaviors. Taking charge of your life again may include getting in touch with your feelings, becoming more assertive, and learning how to ask for what you want or need. You may also want to build a new foundation of security so you become less dependent on getting approval and validation from other people. Many people find added support in twelve-step programs such as Codependents Anonymous, Alcoholics Anonymous, or AlAnon (a support group for anyone who is a family member or friend of a person suffering from an addiction to alcohol).

Hypnotherapy is a form of counseling that helps you explore the link between present reactions and past experiences that may be affecting your responses. Although hypnotherapy includes discussion and insight, it also accesses the intuitive, nonlinear part of the brain. A practitioner uses specific words and suggestions to help you tap into your own inner sources of information. Often called "creative visualization" or "guided visualization" because it uses images and symbols from your imagination, hypnotherapy can enable you to identify old associations that trigger your fears. It can also help you create new mental and emotional patterns that support your freedom and self-confidence. Hypnotherapy helped me to recognize and change the childhood feelings that contributed to my phobias. It also provided a framework to establish positive behavior patterns as I began to approach my fear zones.

Clinicians and researchers continue to explore new technologies for treating anxiety disorders—including panic and phobias, post-traumatic stress, and obsessive-compulsive disorder. Eye Movement Desensitization and Reprocessing (EMDR), originally used with patients suffering from post-traumatic stress, has been effectively used for desensitization with people suffering from panic disorder and phobias. Thought Field Therapy (TFT), a process created by Dr. Roger Callahan, involves tapping specified points on the body to change energy patterns and neutralize the effect of past traumas. It too has helped some people free themselves of phobias. A West Coast doctor has experimented with a virtual reality computer program to work with patients who have a fear of heights. In my experience, these alternative forms of therapy can be a valuable complement to a basic phobia treatment program.

Although your goal is to be independent and self-reliant, you may find that for now you need to rely on other people for *appropriate* support and guidance. Even if putting together the right treatment plan for you initially requires time, effort, and perseverance, the help you get today can strengthen you in the long run. Participating fully in the design of your own program will help you build confidence in your ability to face the challenges of fear and take charge of your life.

How About You?

1. Locating Resources

At first you may feel overwhelmed by the task of locating resources. If you begin systematically, however, you'll soon find choices you never dreamed existed. First survey the health care and health education resources in your area. Check with health centers, hospitals, your health plan, and your doctor or alternative health practitioner.

In your journal, make a list of the resources you have found. List the advantages and disadvantages of each. You may get some leads from the Resources section beginning on page 279.

2. What Is Important to You?

Getting treatment for your phobia is not an end in itself but part of your long-term goals. Focus on the present by making a list of your more immediate goals: to drive on the freeway, to go back to school, and so on.

Next, make a list of your long-term plans. Imagine yourself getting back your life and regaining ground from your phobias. Picture how you want to see yourself in six months, in a year, in five years. Expand on each goal by writing a few paragraphs. Use the present tense, as though you are successfully living your desired life. "It is a year since I got over my fear of flying and I am sitting on the beach in Hawaii . . ." Remember that the small steps you take today are preparation for bigger accomplishments.

5

You Can't Be Relaxed and Anxious at the Same Time

No matter what kind of program you select, the first skill you must develop is the ability to relax. Relaxation is more than putting your feet up. It entails specific physical responses that are the opposite of the emergency responses that cause panic attacks. The physical symptoms of panic are triggered by the secretion of more adrenalin than the body can utilize at that moment. By consciously putting your body in a relaxed state, you can reduce the amount of adrenalin released into your bloodstream and prevent a panic reaction. You can't be relaxed and anxious at the same time.

What Is a Relaxed State?

A relaxed physical state is one in which you are breathing deeply and leisurely, in a way that fills both the chest and abdominal area. Your muscles feel like they have a soft or loose texture, and you may have a sense of melting or a comfortable heaviness or lightness in your body and limbs. Your blood is circulating to all the organs of the body, including the skin, so your complexion has a healthy glow. You may even have a feeling of warmth in your hands and feet.

There is nothing *inherently* wrong with stress. Our bodies are equipped to handle a certain amount of positive and negative stress, excitement, trauma, and fear. In fact, stress can motivate us to focus all our resources on the task at hand, and the additional adrenalin produced can have a beneficial effect on our performance. However, *continued* or *excessive* stress builds up a surplus of adrenalin in the bloodstream. When we are in a state of chronic stress, an overstimulating or anxiety-producing event can push us over our normal threshhold and put us at risk for panic. The result is similar to having four drinks before going to a party and wondering why one glass of wine at your friend's house made you drunk. The glass of wine would have been fine if you started out with no alcohol in your system. Relaxation is the most efficient way to release stress and bring your level of adrenalin back to your normal baseline. Yet many of us don't know how to relax. Some of us are even afraid to relax.

If you are habitually tense, relaxing may feel unfamiliar at first. Some people say they feel more vulnerable when they let down their guard; they associate the feeling of relaxation with losing control. This is one of the paradoxes of panic attacks and anxiety disorders.

You may have coped with your fear, courageously holding on by tensing your body—the very response that signals the body to secrete more adrenalin. This reaction gives the illusion of having some control or offering protection, yet it actually creates a state of readiness for emergency that is out of proportion to the reality of the situation.

Your body has been learning to be uptight for a long time, and it will take some patience and relearning to reverse this pattern. With simple relaxation skills and consistent practice, your body will become accustomed to the alternative of releasing instead of tensing up. To stop having panic attacks you must learn to relax.

Progressive Relaxation

Progressive relaxation gives you the opportunity to acquaint yourself with the difference between tense muscles and relaxed muscles and to shift to the relaxed state at will. The process usually takes about twenty minutes and is easily learned by following a guided audiotape. Some phobia programs and therapists will provide you with a cassette tape to take home. You can also buy a commercial relaxation tape at bookstores or health food stores.

I was introduced to progressive relaxation by Hilda. By the end of our first session I had the reassurance that I was curable, as well as an elementary knowledge of how to breathe deeply and a guided relaxation tape in my pocket. At first it was hard to imagine that my body would really change if I practiced breathing and relaxation, but I was willing to find out for myself.

Choosing a time when I wouldn't be interrupted, I unplugged the phone and loosened my clothing. I chose to lie on a mat on the floor—although a bed, a comfortable chair, or any place where your back and neck are supported is fine. Turning on the tape, I closed my eyes and listened to the directions: "Take a deep breath, fill the lungs, and slowly exhale. Now bend your feet toward your head, tighten the muscles, study the tension, hold it, hold it, and then relax. Feel the tension drain out of your feet into the earth. Now the calves . . ."

Hilda's voice droned on in a friendly, soothing way until I had covered every major muscle group in my body and face. "Now tighten all the little muscles around your mouth, the bridge of your nose, your eyes, and make a prune face. Hold, hold it, and release. Soften around your eyes, slacken your jaw, and let your whole face relax." When I had tensed and released my whole body, I experienced the feeling of sinking into the floor and letting it support me. My shoulders, my back, and my hips seemed to have flattened out, and my breathing was much slower.

Putting Your Mind in a Safe Place

Now that my body was in the rhythm of relaxation, it was time to go to my *safe place.* Hilda's words guided me to choose a place in my imagination that was appealing and comfortable. On the tape, she suggested a tropical beach with warm breezes and invited me to activate all my senses to make it real. "Listen to the sound of the waves lapping against the shore, smell the sea-scented air, feel the gentle sand brush against your skin." I sighed audibly as I imagined myself in the scene. Each day I finished the progressive relaxation by going to my special place.

After a few weeks, my body responded to the word *relax,* and I could go to my special place almost instantly. Just as I had previously learned to activate a stress response in association with a negative image, I now became calm at the recollection of a positive one. The thought of my sandy paradise slowed my heart and made me feel peaceful.

For Brian, imagining his special place was a very effective device. "At first my special place was a favorite vacation spot in the mountains where I had been with Jim. In the beginning, I would picture him there with me. Now I imagine being in my safe place by myself. Just from what I have learned in a few months, I feel more independent. I can actually stop and recognize the tension in my legs or in my back or my neck. In the past, I just lived with it. Now I close my eyes, I think of my special place, breathe deeply, and my body relaxes. I can do it anytime, just by putting my mind in a safe place."

When Brian was at his worst, he canceled a trip to Europe because he could not fly. It was a difficult decision. He and Jim had looked forward to a vacation for a long time and had already bought their tickets and planned their itinerary. "I know it sounds horrible, but

I could not even go on vacation. At my first session I told my therapist, 'Just get me to the point that I can go to Europe and I'll deal with everything else when I get back.'"

As soon as Brian gained enough confidence in his ability to relax, he booked a short flight to Palm Springs. Since his last plane experience had been so devastating, Brian prepared himself carefully for the flight. He felt reassured by the statistics of how safe flying really is and by traveling with his partner. Brian also had skills and helpful distractions to aid him on his return to the scene of his earlier panic. "When I got on the plane, I was able to relax, close my eyes, and put myself in the same safe place I used in my visualization at home. When the plane door shut, I focused my attention on tangible things, like the texture of the seat in front of me, so I wouldn't start thinking about wanting to get off. I had all my supports—chewing gum, a rubber band on my wrist to snap if I started thinking scary thoughts, an antianxiety pill in my pocket as a security measure, and my Sony Walkman. I had my eyes closed, and just when the plane was picking up speed, Jim reached over and touched my elbow. It made everything seem okay."

Not only did Brian rely on his relaxation, but he also distracted himself from thinking fear-provoking thoughts by keeping his mind busy listening to music. "For most of the trip I had my headphones on and was playing music really loud. Jim thought I was listening to my relaxation tape the whole time and was surprised to find out it was Neil Young. I actually enjoyed that flight."

The more often you practice relaxation and breathing, the more accessible it will be to you in a potentially anxiety-producing situation. Brian had trained his body to relax and stay that way, whether he was listening to his relaxation tape or his favorite music. "When you have a positive experience like that, it gives you the confidence to go on. I needed that." After a few more short practice flights, Brian was able to make new plans to go to Europe.

Deep Breathing

Take a moment now to notice how you are feeling as you read this. You may be excited about getting information that can help you. You may be uncomfortable because the very subject makes you anxious. Observe what is happening in your body. How do your shoulders feel? Is your jaw tight or relaxed? Is your belly tense or at ease? Is your breathing deep and full, or is it shallow and restricted to your upper chest? If you are not sure, you can put one hand on your belly and one on your chest and breathe normally. Notice which hand moves the most.

Few of us breathe fully. Often our breathing habits stem from earliest childhood or even infancy, when tensing our stomach muscles and holding our breath was our first defense against stimuli and sensations that affected our tender bodies. We also learned to block our feelings by holding our breath. It gave us some control over our response to an overwhelming environment. When under stress, we often revert to breathing only in the upper chest. Unfortunately, this keeps our bodies tense and signals the brain that something is threatening and we'd better gear up for a potential emergency. That triggers an excess of adrenalin, which in turn causes uncomfortable sensations. We respond by holding our breath even more. Mastering deep, diaphragmatic breathing can convert the panic cycle to a calming cycle.

Deep breathing was one of the most important skills that Kathy learned to reduce her panic response. "When I told myself I might lose control, my stomach got so constricted that I couldn't relax it enough to take a breath. My chest was gripped with fear, and I got dizzy. The feeling of dizziness scares me. I've never fainted, yet I always thought, 'What if I faint? Will I keep breathing?'"

When Kathy learned that her shallow breathing was giving emergency messages to her brain, she thought she couldn't change her breathing pattern because the feelings of panic came on so quickly. It took her several months of practicing relaxation and breathing before she experienced the big difference it could make. One day, when out with her daughter, she challenged the panic by staying with her deep breathing. "I forced myself to look around and take deep, slow breaths. I had to put all my concentration on it, and that was hard for me. I focused on my breath and the air—feeling it, smelling it, and noticing the fragrances in the air. To my amazement, I calmed down. The breathing really helps me out."

Try It Yourself

Breathe intentionally by pushing your belly out with each inhalation, filling first the lower abdomen, then the belly, then the upper chest. You can imagine that the lungs are a balloon that fills your whole body and you are pushing out every little wrinkle. You may notice that as the lungs fill with air, they push the diaphragm down and the lower abdomen expands. For this reason, deep breathing is sometimes called *abdominal* or *diaphragmatic breathing.* When you exhale, first collapse the upper chest, then suck your belly inward so you empty the lungs completely. Count slowly from one to four with each inhalation and exhalation. After several minutes, let your breathing return to its natural rhythm.

It is important not to hyperventilate, because hyperventilation decreases the supply of carbon dioxide in your lungs and can make you feel lightheaded. Should this happen, breathe into a paper bag to restore the proper balance. Once you know what it feels like to breathe fully, you will notice the times during your day when you are hardly taking in any air. As soon as you become aware of this shallow breath pattern, make a shift to abdominal breathing. With conscious attention, deeper breathing becomes natural and will become easier to do whenever you feel your body tense or your thoughts turn to fear.

Using the Anxiety Scale

Bonnie combined two techniques to reduce her chance of having a panic attack. She had practiced her relaxation at home so many times that her body knew the procedure automatically. One day when she was driving on the freeway, she started to feel the first signals of anxiety. "The minute I noticed myself getting tense, I went through my body, mentally scanning each part and relaxing it. I did the relaxation so many times at home that I could do it in the car at will, instantly. It worked. The anxiety seeped away." She also had learned to rate the early signs of tension in her body and had used the *anxiety scale* to identify and lessen her anxiety in its early stages.

The anxiety scale rates physical stress symptoms from zero to ten. It helps you distinguish the symptoms that are merely uncomfortable from those that feel intolerable. *Zero* means no anxiety—literally, no sweat. Ratings from *one* to *three* represent an increase in physical symptoms: muscle tension, sweaty palms, butterflies in the stomach, slightly increased heart rate, shallow breathing. *Four* represents marked anxiety, an intensifying of symptoms. At this stage you may doubt that you can continue to cope. *Five* and *six* represent a mild to moderate panic attack with increased disorientation. From level *five* up to *ten,* the exaggerated sensations and fearful thoughts often provoke the feeling that you must escape from the situation. The exact sensations vary from person to person, and there are many symptoms you may never have. As you observe your own reactions, you can make an anxiety scale that describes your levels of arousal. My anxiety scale looks like this:

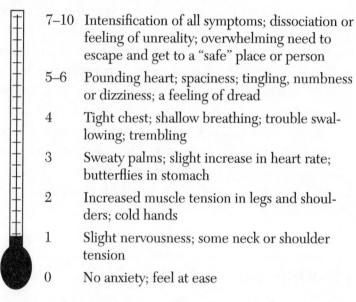

7–10   Intensification of all symptoms; dissociation or feeling of unreality; overwhelming need to escape and get to a "safe" place or person

5–6   Pounding heart; spaciness; tingling, numbness or dizziness; a feeling of dread

4   Tight chest; shallow breathing; trouble swallowing; trembling

3   Sweaty palms; slight increase in heart rate; butterflies in stomach

2   Increased muscle tension in legs and shoulders; cold hands

1   Slight nervousness; some neck or shoulder tension

0   No anxiety; feel at ease

If you notice that your hands are cold or sweaty, your shoulders tense, or your breathing tight, the scale offers a standard to help you interpret your symptoms realistically. Instead of thinking, "Oh, no, I'm going to have a panic attack!" you can reassure yourself that this is only a level two or three, and you know how to lower your tension level. Give your body the signal to relax. Soften your belly and take a deep breath. Raise your shoulders to your ears, then drop them down with a sigh. Breathe in and breathe out. Tell yourself that you are okay. Observe yourself going back down to level one or zero and then continue with what you were doing.

In the past you may not have had the information or experience to recognize the early stages of anxiety, so if you felt panic-stricken, you felt as though everything happened all at once and without warning. With an awareness of relative levels of arousal, you don't need to wait until your heart feels like it's bursting and you want to flee the situation. You can use your relaxation techniques, along with cognitive skills described in the next chapter, to reduce the anxiety and prevent escalation to higher levels. You will discover a balance point where you are able to tolerate some discomfort in order to challenge your fear. By using your tools to stay in the situation longer, you will discover that you can take care of yourself.

Floating, Not Fighting

Bonnie found that if she didn't resist the panic, it lost its momentum. "I read that you could face the panic by saying 'Okay, go ahead, do your thing; I don't care.' I didn't think I would ever be able to do that. Then one day I tried it when my anxiety was beginning to build. I just accepted my symptoms, didn't struggle, and the panic dissolved by itself."

Bonnie was using a process first described by Dr. Claire Weekes, who coined the word *floating*. Forcing yourself creates more tension, but if you think of yourself *floating forward without resistance*, like floating on a wave or a cloud, you release tension and consequently reduce your panic symptoms. Dr. Weekes describes this as "relaxation with action," encouraging clients to float through situations that intimidate them. When you accept the sensations, allow the time for the feelings of discomfort to pass, and you don't permit fearful thoughts to stimulate production of more adrenalin, your body returns to its natural state of balance.

Nurturing Your Nervous System

Relaxation and breathing are the basic physical building blocks of reducing panic responses. There are other ways to calm your nervous system, such as biofeedback, martial arts, yoga, and meditation. I found out that my health plan covered biofeedback and decided to try it.

Biofeedback teaches you to recognize the subtle, inner shifts that raise or lower your tension level. Usually an electronic device is used to monitor your level of stress. In my sessions, sensors were taped to my fingertips to measure the secretion of sweat as an indication of my anxiety level. This measurement is called the *galvanic skin response*. My fluctuating response levels were conveyed to me by an audio tone, which increased in volume as my anxiety rose and decreased as it fell. It was my job to keep the sound low and steady.

I was amazed to discover that I actually could control my body's response through inner shifts, sometimes so subtle that I couldn't describe exactly what I had done. In addition to using abdominal breathing, I learned to expand, soften, release, and relax. Once I knew how this felt inside me, I could access this method again in my daily life. Some biofeedback systems show the response with a graph on a computer screen rather than through sound.

Martial arts or other practices that combine mental concentration with physical control can also affect the nervous system. Yoga strengthens the body and makes it more flexible. It also provides specific poses that tone the parasympathetic nervous system. For example, forward bends have a calming influence on the nerves and even affect glands such as the adrenals. After going to a yoga class for six months, my nerves seemed less raw and I had a new reference point for what "relaxed" felt like in my own body. I knew which poses helped me feel "grounded" or solid on my feet, which is the opposite of feeling disconnected or dissociated from my body when panic-stricken. Other mind-body practices such as t'ai chi and aikido can have a similar effect. Some people find that acupuncture has a calming effect on the nervous system.

Meditation and Centering

Meditation has long been used by Eastern religions as a way to seek the realization of truth. In the past decades it has become increasingly popular in the West, not only as part of a spiritual path but because of its great value in counteracting stress and helping people find inner peace in the midst of life's complexities.

What is commonly called meditation in the West may refer to a wide variety of experiences, including silent concentration, watching your breathing or thoughts, following a guided visualization, focusing your attention on a specific area such as the heart, or self-hypnosis. Whatever form you are drawn to, meditation is a practical tool that can help you feel calmer. It need not be connected with any religion or spiritual path.

In her phobia group, Alicia acquired insights that relieved her worry that she had upset others or that they were thinking badly of her. She deepened her feelings of calm and safety by taking an adult education class at the local community center, where she learned techniques for turning inward and centering herself. These complemented her relaxation skills, reduced her fear of panic, and made her feel more confident in approaching situations that were previously phobic for her.

"I don't know why they didn't offer meditation as part of the phobia class," she told me. "I see all these things as interconnected—breathing, relaxation, and the ability to let the worry go and concentrate on just being here in the moment. When I have panic attacks, my tendency is to feel as though I'm coming apart. The meditation and grounding make me feel that I'm here and not flitting out someplace else. It surprised me that I could relax so deeply."

Alicia's meditation class always started with slow, deep breathing, inhaling and exhaling while counting to eight. Besides that, Alicia learned several techniques that helped her feel more connected to the earth. "We learned the bear position. You stand solid like a bear, placing your feet apart, bending your knees slightly, and feeling your center of gravity. It struck me that what we

were doing was putting aside all worries while grounding and relaxing at the same time. You can do it anytime—before taking a walk or going to class. I also
learned that I could add a visualization if I felt apprehensive about driving. I imagined surrounding myself
with a protective white light, grounding my car and
myself. By doing this, I felt calmer when I got in my car
to go out."

Alicia also found that after even a brief meditation
she had a different relationship to things around her.
"One day after doing the bear position and slow breathing, we went outside and were told to focus on something in nature. Because I was so relaxed I had a different feeling about things in my environment. I noticed
exactly what was happening around me. There were
clouds in the sky, and I got the feeling that they were
very comforting. They were like a blanket over all of us.
Now I always see the clouds as comforting. Even rain
clouds or storm clouds make me feel comfortable and
secure." Part of the value of any meditation or centering practice is that changing your inner state alters the
way you view everything outside of you.

Meditation was initially intimidating to me
because I thought of myself as a restless person who
couldn't do it right. When I tried to sit still, my back
ached, my foot fell asleep, my ear itched. My thoughts
wandered and I couldn't quiet my mind. As I sat on my
pillow, I planned what I would eat for lunch, tried to
remember where I left my sweater, and wondered if I
would have time to pick up my photos at the drugstore.

In a book called *Peace Is Every Step,* I found a practice of meditation that allowed me to use my thoughts to bring me back to peacefulness. It is called *mindfulness meditation,* and was introduced to the West by a Vietnamese Buddhist teacher named Thich Nhat Hanh. His method helps you become calm and present by accompanying your activity with a simple descriptive verse such as: "Breathing in, I calm my body. Breathing out, I smile." You can use these words or create your own phrase to describe any ordinary situation, such as washing dishes. "Breathing in, I feel the warm soapy water. Breathing out, I feel calm." It's a good idea to practice each day while sitting quietly in a chair, but it can also be very useful as a "meditation in the marketplace." This combination of mindfulness and breathing is an effective way to reduce anxiety while stopped in traffic or waiting for your name to be called in class. It helped me get through my first plane flight.

Breathing In, I Calm My Body and My Mind . . .

I used to love the adventure of traveling, until my fear of flying cut into my pleasure as well as my relationship to my family back east. After seeing how much more confident I felt driving when I used breathing and relaxation techniques, I decided I was ready to fly again. I "flew" first in my easy chair, staying relaxed while visualizing the ride to the airport, checking in at the ticket counter, getting on the airplane, remaining calm in my seat during take-off and arriving at my destination, greeted by the open arms of a friend. As I imagined each of these events, I learned to lower my body tension and relax.

My actual flight from San Francisco to San Diego was only an hour long, but in anticipation I had diarrhea for several days before. I was scared. But I also chose to trust my tools. Once on the flight, I used my deep breathing and relaxation techniques. What most helped me thwart fearful thoughts was the meditation practice I had learned. I was able to detach from my fearful thoughts by repeating "Breathing in, I calm my body and my mind. Breathing out, I feel peaceful." I held my copy of *Peace Is Every Step* on my lap for good luck!

As I closed my eyes, I got an image of the faces of the people from my phobia group: Alicia, Lew, Carol . . . They all seemed to be rooting for me. My heart melted open. My anxiety faded. I *could* do it! "Breathing in, I calm . . ." I wanted to do it for me and for them. I wanted us all to be free.

If you already are comfortable with a meditation practice, you may want to make it part of your daily routine. If you have never tried meditation, I suggest taking a class, picking up a book or guided tape, or just doing what I call "no-fault" meditation. Reserve twenty minutes to do nothing but breathe and relax. Whatever happens in that period is good enough. When you notice the thoughts, bring your awareness to the next in-breath. If you spend most of the time thinking about your life, accept that without judgment. There's no "wrong way" to do no-fault meditation.

Reviewing Your Lifestyle Habits

There are some basic lifestyle habits that can reduce the overstimulation of your nervous system. Daily exercise is a way of using up extra adrenalin. Have you ever noticed that after you dance or work out, your mind seems quieter than before? Just twenty to thirty minutes a day of exercise such as walking, bike riding, or low-impact aerobics can make you feel calmer. In addition, exercise can help you get accustomed to a more rapid heartbeat, thus making this symptom less alarming. Alicia begins each day with very vigorous dancing. Kathy uses working in her garden and strenuous housecleaning as forms of exercise.

Changes in diet can also make a big difference. Reducing stimulants—particularly caffeine, nicotine, and sugar—minimizes the swings in energy and mood that can trigger a nervous response. Eating a well-balanced, healthy diet can reduce your physical predisposition to stress. One friend told me that when she started eating a diet low in sugar and based primarily on grains and vegetables, she felt her mind become calmer. For the first time she could hear her fearful thoughts and have time to stop them before her body reacted. We are not all equally sensitive, but it's sensible to evaluate the foods you eat and drink and to cut back on the things that overstimulate your nervous system.

A.A. participants use a simple rule to reduce stress to the nervous system. The H.A.L.T. rule says, "Don't get too Hungry, too Angry, too Lonely, or too Tired." I find these same reminders apply to my sensitive nervous system. When I let my blood sugar drop, I feel "spaced out" and less grounded. I found that having some protein at each meal keeps me feeling more steady. I also carry some nourishment, either a few crackers or a high-energy bar. If I hold back my feelings or don't express my needs, my tension builds up. It's important for me to communicate even if I can't always have things the way I wish. If I feel isolated or separate from others, my mind starts to drift toward fearful thoughts. It helps to call a friend just to have human contact. And when I get too tired, my nervous system is not able to handle problems as well as when I am rested.

Does relaxing and taking care of your nervous system sound time-consuming to you? Yes, it can be, but not nearly as time-consuming as the hours, days, and months spent worrying about things that never happen. Remember, you can start with making small changes and gradually integrate new habits into your life. A woman in one of the programs I attended complained at the end of the first class that she couldn't believe she paid hundreds of dollars to learn how to breathe. Several months later, as we chatted after class, she confided, "That breathing has made such a difference. If I didn't learn another thing in this class, that would have been worth it."

How About You?

1. Pay Attention to Your Breathing

For one day, pay attention to your breathing. Don't try to change it or control it—just observe it. In your journal, jot down what was going on when you noticed yourself holding your breath. What were you doing? What were you thinking?

In the following days, when you notice yourself restricting your breathing, follow the directions in the section called "Try It Yourself" (page 89) to breathe more fully and deeply in your abdomen.

2. Relax

Start a regular relaxation practice of some kind. You can use the instructions beginning on page 283 to make your own tape, you can buy a tape, or go to a yoga or stress reduction class. It's best to have something you do every day for at least fifteen minutes.

3. Exercise

Exercise relieves anxious feelings by burning up accumulated adrenalin. If you're not used to regular exercise, start slowly. Exercise does not have to be extremely vigorous to have an effect on your body. Walking can be as beneficial as bicycling or jogging. Work up to exercising every day for twenty to thirty minutes.

6

You Can Change Your Mind

Thoughts trigger physical responses in the body. Imagine taking a fresh lemon, slicing it into thick, juicy slivers, and squeezing droplets of the sour liquid into your mouth. Perhaps you already notice a slight quivering of the salivary glands under your tongue. The memory of a lemon slice stimulated your glandular response. Pleasant and comforting thoughts can bring an involuntary smile to your lips. Frightening thoughts can trigger your emergency alarm system and stimulate the secretion of adrenalin. Yet your fearful thoughts are rarely an accurate reflection of reality. They are learned habits that have become as automatic and unconscious as how you hold your pen or how you walk. In order to stop *being* phobic, you must stop *thinking* phobic.

"Brain in a Bag"

In teaching the Phobease class, Dr. Liebgold illustrates our relationship to fear thoughts by holding up a display he calls "brain in a bag." Every time someone in the class uses anxiety-producing words to describe an experience, he rattles a brown paper bag with a rubber model of a brain in it. "I went to the store and there were *hordes* (rattle, rattle) of people coming at me." "The traffic was so *jammed* (rattle) that the people in the next car could *stare* (rattle) at me for hours." "It's such an *overwhelming* (rattle, rattle) job that I'll *never* (rattle) get it done on time."

Like the brain in the paper bag, your own brain can't see what is in front of you, and must rely on what you tell it to decide if your life is in danger. If you use dramatic words, if you describe minor inconveniences as catastrophic events, or if you tell yourself that others judge you and find you lacking, your brain gets rattled and puts in an order for adrenalin.

The information you give to your brain can affect the intensity or duration of a panic episode. The first stage of anxiety may be triggered by a common stressor such as noise, traffic, or crowding. The second stage, or escalation of symptoms, stems from your interpretation of the original symptoms or situation. To stop scaring yourself into a panic, you must separate what is actually happening from the thoughts that rattle your brain. For example, the fact is that traffic is at a standstill and you can't do anything about it. You think: *There must be a terrible accident; what if there are people and blood all over the road; I'll die; I'm never going to get home.*

Your subjective interpretations distort the objective reality. Unchecked, they can provoke new distressing sensations or prolong and intensify the initial ones.

When you identify your fear-provoking words and thoughts, you can change them to realistic, supportive messages. *I might get home a little late because of this traffic, so I'll just relax and turn on the radio.*

Recognizing Fear Thoughts

The thoughts that set off our internal alarm can be called *fear thoughts*. Fear thoughts tend to appear as descriptive words or phrases that trigger your worst fears—*huge, tiny, alone, crowded, stuck, trapped, stared at, laughed at, fail, fall, frozen.* Fear thoughts tell you to look for everything that could go wrong; they exaggerate potential danger; they anticipate future trouble; they remind you of past failures and disappointments; they thrive on self-talk that is overly critical and demanding of perfection; and they turn ordinary events into catastrophes.

Most terrifying of all, the fear of *What People Think* (WPT) threatens you with humiliation and rejection. It is natural to care about your relationships with others; all people have some concern about how other people respond to them. But many of us exaggerate the importance of others' opinions and judgments. If worrying about the possible thoughts of total strangers prevents you from going to public places, you may be frightening yourself with the WPTs.

When Hilda first asked me if I worried about what other people were thinking, I didn't see what her question had to do with my driving anxiety. I insisted that my only concern was that I physically couldn't control the car. But once the WPTs were brought to my attention, I noticed that I spent a lot of time looking in my rearview mirror, wondering if the driver behind me was irritated about my speed or my performance. I didn't want strangers in an elevator to see me grip the handrail, and I felt self-conscious about chewing my food when eating in a restaurant with anyone I didn't know well.

Fearful thinking is often learned from the environment in which we grow up. A participant in a group I attended remembered her childhood as a daily crisis. "Even good events were traumatic," she told us. "Going on vacation to our beach house in the summer became a nightmare of worries and problems." If you come from a family where everything was a drama, where you didn't feel protected, or where feelings could not be openly expressed, you may be accustomed to imagining potential danger in every situation. Once you develop the habit of *catastrophizing,* you may lose your ability to discriminate between a minor problem and a major crisis. Your child arriving home from school ten minutes late or a car accident miles away can generate as much of a frenzy as if your house were on fire. Catastrophic thinking raises your level of adrenalin.

Shrink the "Phoboo"

When Howard first learned the skills to conquer his phobias, he wrote an imaginative story about stopping fear thoughts. He personified these thoughts in a character called the Phoboo. The Phoboo lives on scare juice built up by anxiety-producing thoughts. "You're a long way from home," shrieks the Phoboo in cartoon form. "Elevators are so small you can hardly get enough air." "If you open your mouth, nothing will come out." And of course, the Phoboo creates masterpieces for keeping anxiety flowing: "People will know how scared you are." "You're a sissy." "You'll never get well." "You'll die."

Howard goes on to describe how he learned to shrink the Phoboo by not giving him the words that made him feel so big and important. Every time a scary, catastrophic, or doom-and-gloom thought appeared, Howard used his favorite *thought-stopping* technique. STOP!— deep breath—1-2-3-4—exhale—I CAN HANDLE IT. He then substituted a pleasant thought (bonus, vacation). When Howard practiced this thought-stopping and thought-substituting technique regularly, the Phoboo couldn't get enough scare juice (adrenalin) to become threatening. "Robbed of his scare juices, he shriveled to virtually nothing. Although he tried mightily, he never *booed* (that's the cry of the Phoboo) loud enough to be taken seriously again."

When Experience Misleads Us

False beliefs often provide the foundation for fearful thinking habits. These beliefs seem like facts because they grow out of real experiences that had significant emotional impact. Yet, the general conclusion we draw from these experiences is often not accurate.

My kindergarten teacher *did* ridicule me when I nervously jumped up and down instead of sitting in my seat. My mother *did* get very upset when I had a temper tantrum in front of her new friend. The conclusion I drew—that I must always control my feelings and that I would be humiliated or punished if I showed anger or strong emotion—was plausible in my childhood. But I didn't limit that belief to my childhood situation. I thought my emotional security depended on staying in control, not only to please my teacher and my mother, but with *every* person and in *every* situation. I believed that if I let down my guard, something unacceptable might leak out. Although I didn't think of the original incidents when similar situations arose, my brain, performing its hundred thousand computations per second, wired my false beliefs into my rules of conduct. Until I learned to test my belief against reality, my brain registered any situation that resembled the original incident as dangerous. As a result I valued the ability to control or suppress my emotions and became accustomed to an inner rigidity that added to my level of tension.

Alicia traces her discomfort in social situations to the criticism and humiliation she experienced in childhood. "I hear people talk about their critical parents, but my fears of what people are thinking seem more connected to the impact of my relationship with my sister. She was seven years older than me, and as children we didn't get along. I remember one Thanksgiving in particular. We were at my aunt's house and after a big dinner, she brought out the pie. She asked me if I wanted some, and I said 'Sure.' Then my sister shouted in this *booming* voice, 'I can't believe you're having dessert after all that dinner you ate!' I felt everyone staring at me. My face got all hot." This incident left an indelible impression on Alicia, but it was only one of many instances in which she felt attacked for how she looked, for something she did, or for something she said.

Alicia's anxiety about being ridiculed continued to affect her behavior as she got older. "In school I intentionally cultivated a soft voice so if I said the wrong thing, no one would hear me." Her childhood experience became the basis for a false belief about the danger of exposing her thoughts and feelings. It became so rooted in her outlook that it produced a fear response in her body even when she was an adult going into a social situation, such as having dinner with friends.

In the phobia group Alicia took risks that allowed her to evaluate her assumptions against her actual experience. As she discovered that other people respected her viewpoints, she learned to distinguish her conditioned fear thoughts—the WPTs that sprang from the past—from her realistic observations of the current situation.

Several months after completing the group, she took an intern position at a local company. Six years had passed since she had left her last job, and she hoped as an intern she would be under less pressure. "It was very difficult for me. I had a couple of panic attacks when I went into the boss's office to talk to her or when I sat in on staff meetings. There was absolutely nothing threatening there, but I felt extraordinarily ill at ease."

With the skills she learned, Alicia was able to tolerate her uncomfortable feelings because she had a different attitude toward them. "Now I know that the feelings will pass if I breathe and don't fight them. I used to say to myself, 'I wish I were dead rather than having to go through this.' Now I say, 'I'll be glad when this passes.' I stuck it out, and when I thought about it later I said to myself, 'I *did* do it. I *did* go in there, I *did* talk to people even though I felt uncomfortable.'" Alicia loosened the grip of her phobia by giving herself credit for every accomplishment.

Another victory for Alicia was the completion of a major project. "I had to make phone calls to other cities to get information. That was hard for me when I started, but it got easier after a while." By talking to herself in a reassuring way, Alicia was able to convince her "brain in a bag" that other people, even strangers, could be supportive. "If you say, 'I could use some help. Do you have this information?' they talk to you for a long time or they mail you information. Most people are helpful—though I had to get through my discomfort to reaffirm that."

No matter how difficult our past experiences have been, we are further handicapped when we stick to rigid rules and beliefs that are based on a very limited perspective. Every time we take the opportunity to confront and test our old beliefs, we increase our options. Challenging fearful beliefs is not always easy, but it is necessary in order to become free of panic and phobias.

A Fear Avalanche

We often use our active imaginations in the service of fear. We think of possibilities that another person would never imagine. We expect traffic jams, terminal illnesses, and potentially embarrassing moments because we are in the habit of scaring ourselves. Even the way we phrase a question can set us up for anxiety. We ask, "What if I eat in a restaurant and my throat closes up and I can't swallow and everyone stares at me and sees me lose control?" or, "What if there is turbulence and one of the plane's engines dies and we drop thousands of feet and . . . ?" If we do hear of a plane crash or overhear a disparaging remark, we take it as proof that our fears are realistic.

A *fear avalanche* is a chain of frightening thoughts or expectations, each built on the previous imagined event. Like an avalanche, it picks up power and speed as it progresses. Kathy's panic attacks often began with an initial flush of body heat, which was then fueled by her thoughts: "I'm going to faint. What's going to happen if I pass out? What if people think I'm crazy? How much worse can I get?" Yet not one of these possibilities ever materialized. Kathy got dizzy but never fainted. Her knees trembled, but she could always walk until she got to a familiar place. She was horrified at the thought of what people might think, but no one seemed to notice her distress.

I was an expert at creating fear avalanches. Whenever I felt anxious while driving, I imagined that at any minute I would lose control and my hands would fly off the steering wheel; the car would go careening into other lanes or fling itself over the edge. I made my heart pound as I imagined the sensation of spinning around in traffic.

But as terrified as I was, as tense as I got, I never let go of the steering wheel. No matter how uncomfortable I felt, my fears never materialized. I always had enough control to steer, stop, or get to a place that seemed safe. One day I did pull over to the side and started crying. After a few minutes, I decided that nothing could be worse than sitting there thinking about the drive, so I did my standard thought-stopping technique. Remembering my calming breath, I inhaled deeply, held it for the count of four, and, exhaling, said, "I can do it." Switching on my flashers to alert other drivers that I was going slower than the rest of the traffic, I maneuvered back into traffic, driving about twenty-five miles an hour until I reached my destination. Although my body was exhausted by the exertion of dealing with so much fear, the actual driving was fine, almost meditative, as I repeated slowly and calmly, "I can do it."

A fear avalanche interferes with the natural recovery cycle. Without this "second scare," the body gradually winds down from the physiological effect of surplus adrenalin. The cascade of fear thoughts prolongs and intensifies the panic reaction. But many people are convinced that their fearful thoughts somehow protect them. They believe that if they stop thinking of what they fear, and let down their guard, the worst possibility would catch them unprepared. This belief gives a magical power to fear thoughts. It is sensible to assess a situation and take realistic precautions. *But worry is not preparation.* It gives the illusion that you are preparing yourself when, in fact, the only thing fear thoughts prepare you for is panic.

Stopping Fear Thoughts

One of the first tasks in reducing or eliminating the physical sensations of panic is to stop the fear avalanche before it gains momentum. Having learned to relax on cue, Bonnie realized that to keep her anxiety down, she would have to stop her fear thoughts. "I believe that my thoughts were the source of my agoraphobia. I had gotten to the point where I always was negative and fearful. The thoughts I had were so irrational that I didn't dare tell anyone what I was thinking. All of my What If thoughts involved some physical harm to myself. I used to run at an indoor track with a railing around it and a basketball court down below. I kept thinking that I'd fall down into this court or that I'd be scalded by hot water in the shower."

By listening to her lessons on cassettes, Bonnie acquired skills that prevented these thoughts from taking root in her mind. "I didn't let a thought stay in my mind. If it did, it would develop, it would grow. The suggested technique was to interrupt these thoughts the minute they started by saying, 'I am getting better and I am getting over this.' I would say it over and over again until my mind got bored and got another thought that was acceptable and nonthreatening. I credit the progressive muscle relaxation and thought stopping as the keys to my getting better."

The repetition of a reassuring thought can stop and replace an avalanche of fear thoughts. You *must* immediately interrupt your habitual fear-thought pattern with the same words and same action *every* time. A common technique is the one I used in my car. Say to yourself out loud, "STOP!" Then take a long breath, hold it for the count of four (1-2-3-4). As you exhale, say, "I can handle it." STOP! can become as automatic as your braking response to a red light or a stop sign. This is usually followed by a phrase such as *I can handle it, I am getting better, I am getting over this, This will pass,* or even, *So what? Who cares?* The exact words you choose don't matter so much as being consistent. Your body is always listening. You can teach it to accept these words as a signal that there is no emergency.

Don't Leave Me Alone with My Thoughts

Any *distraction* can interrupt your fear-thought pattern. You can use a physical stimulus such as snapping a rubber band on your wrist for a quick shift of attention. You can play a tape, sing a song, whistle, or take a drink of water. Count the bricks in a wall or the pickup trucks on the road. You can change the radio station, estimate the height and length of the checkout counter, read signs, spell words, add numbers. Any activity that requires logical, rational thinking shifts your reference point from the right brain, where emotional responses such as fear have their origin, to the left hemisphere, the seat of logic.

This approach, also called *cortical thinking*, has sustained me through countless drives. One day when I felt the first flutters in my stomach, I started my addition. "Two plus two equals four. Four and two make six. Six and two . . ." My body shifted into neutral, and by the time I got to forty-four, I was home. Another time, while riding with a friend, I put all my attention on an interesting story she was telling me. When she lapsed into silence, I felt my mind drift back to my What If thoughts. "Please keep talking," I begged her. "Don't leave me alone with my thoughts for one second!" Distraction works best at the early stages of discomfort. Using the anxiety scale to rate your symptoms, you can focus on logical thoughts at the first sign of tension.

After you interrupt your fear thoughts, it's a good idea to keep your mind busy with a positive replacement thought, either your usual saying such as *I can do it*, or a supportive thought such as *I've done this before; I can do it again*. Then anchor yourself in tangible reality. Look around and see where you are. In a restaurant, notice that other people are sitting and eating. In your car, touch the upholstery of your seat. Feel the texture. Outside, look at the shape of the leaves on trees, smell the roses, hear the children's voices. When you take a calm inventory of what is around you, your brain believes that you are safe.

When I drive, I carry a small survival kit of sensory attractions and distractions. It includes crackers, a container of water, a music or guided relaxation tape, and a small bottle of an aromatic herb solution (a form of aromatherapy) that gives me pleasure. I smell the lavender.

I look at the white triangles of sailboats in the bay. I feel
the smooth plastic of my steering wheel. I listen atten-
tively to the words of my favorite bridge-crossing song,
"Bridges of Love."

When I first became aware of my fear thoughts, I
believed that I had to actively fight them with one of
these simple techniques. Over time it has become more
natural for me to just remove my focus from them.
When I give them no energy, they seem to drift to the
background of my mind and dissipate. I can bring to
the foreground what is real and tangible. When you
keep your attention on what is here, you can't scare
yourself with fantasy thoughts.

Introducing Claire:
Describing the Feelings

Claire learned that she could reduce her anxiety and
panic by facing the feelings rather than listening to her
own fear-provoking thoughts. She is in her late twenties
and has a very close relationship with her husband, Ray.
Though she earns a living coordinating a job training
program, her real passion is for creative writing. She is
enthusiastic and motivated, convinced that she can
learn from every experience.

Claire's phobias date back to her teens. She still
remembers the kind of thoughts that filled her with terror. "In my late teens I was practicing for a play and the
lights went out. Everyone else in the room was laughing, and I started fantasizing that there was someone in

the room and I was in danger and couldn't escape. I think that was the first time I had the feeling of needing to flee. Then, in my twenties, when at my husband's side in the grocery store I might suddenly think, 'I have to leave right now; I can't stay in here.' I didn't understand what was going on in my body so I would manufacture some logical, external reason to explain why I needed to leave the store. 'That person looks like he is going to rob the store.' 'I sense danger; it must be because that woman over there is going to do something terrible.' I would tell my husband my suspicions, but I never talked about how I felt inside."

Claire believes she would have gone through the rest of her life scaring herself and depending heavily on her husband had she not injured her shoulder while playing water polo. The X ray of Claire's injured shoulder revealed two unexplained masses. When she began to undergo tests to determine whether she had a tumor, her panic reached crisis proportions.

"Though it turned out I didn't have cancer, I was going through tests for almost a year. One of the necessary tests was an MRI. They slowly move your whole body through a piece of equipment shaped like a tube. I went into this machine, just after playing an exhausting water polo tournament. I was in layers of sweat clothes, the fan wasn't on, and there was barely any room for air to pass back and forth. I went in with my eyes closed and was fine for about three minutes. Then a sensation that I still can't find words for started at the bottom of my toes and became a wave of overwhelming terror."

The technician brought Claire out of the tube and convinced her to start over. He assured her that the fan would be turned on and that he would take her out at any point if she wanted to stop. The third time, Claire agreed to take a tranquilizer. "By that time I felt I trusted the technician. I was two-thirds through the test when I had a panic attack. I said, 'I need to come out now,' and he said, 'No.' I said, 'I want to come out now; you promised.' My voice was getting smaller, and he said, 'Now Claire, be a good girl.' Ray came over immediately; I could feel his arms on my legs. He was getting ready to pull me out when the technician released me. I refused to go in there and feel *that* again."

Claire never completed the MRI, but she discovered that she could calm herself by describing what she was *feeling*. "I discovered I could talk about exactly what I was feeling and identify the exact sensations, rather than invent a reason or thought to justify my nervous apprehension. I began looking at what was going on *in me* rather than putting my focus on something *out there*. When I did that, the sensations went away."

Instead of fighting the panic or making up a story about it, Claire turned to face it. She was surprised that she felt safer by talking directly and frankly about the symptoms as they were happening. This was Claire's way of "floating." When you accept the symptoms without adding a negative internal dialogue, they complete their cycle and recede. By staying with her body, not her fear thoughts, Claire began to disarm the power of panic.

Claire had to be assertive to convince her health plan to refer her to a therapist who focused on anxiety-related problems. Her self-exploration in these sessions helped her recognize when accumulated stress set off her anxiety. "I may go up and down escalators for four months with no problem, and then all of a sudden I'll dread stepping onto one. I'll have the thought, 'I'm going to throw myself off the escalator and kill myself.' When that happens I now answer realistically, 'No, Claire, that's not what this is about. You've had a hard day, a busy week, and you didn't sleep very well. What would be the best way to take care of yourself?'" Claire always gives herself a choice about whether she wants to go further or retreat. "I may stand at the escalator until I feel calm and then get on it. Sometimes I'll just laugh and realize the fear thoughts are just a habit. Most of the time I will take the hand of the little girl inside me who is pleading, 'Please take care of me.' I reassure her that I'm there for her, and we go up the escalator together."

Learning to Think Realistically

Hilda proved to me that there was an alternative to my accustomed way of thinking by showing me a new model. One day while we were driving, she encouraged me to move out of the right lane and drive in the middle lane. "But Hilda," I lamented, "the right lane is my safe lane. I need to stay in the right lane in case I need to pull off." Hilda challenged my logic and showed me a more realistic way to think.

"Tell me exactly what you are thinking."

"I'm thinking that if I get anxious and need to pull off, there might be a car in the right lane, and I won't be able to get over."

"How long do you think that car will be in your way?"

"I guess a few seconds or even a few minutes."

"So, you'll breathe slowly and deeply as you've been practicing and put on your signal. The cars behind you will see that you want to pull over, and in a minute, you'll get in the right lane."

"Oh, I never thought of it that way."

I tested out her version of reality by practicing changing lanes. It was true. It often took only seconds for me to get into the right lane. Hilda insists that most drivers are careful, conscientious, and considerate. Now I appreciate all the patient and courteous drivers, instead of focusing all my attention on the occasional rude one. Hilda has also convinced me that while it is important to drive safely, it is not my responsibility to make other drivers happy. When I start to get the WPTs, the memory of Hilda's voice comes back to me: "If they don't like how you're driving, what are they going to do about it? They can pass you, they can be impatient. Their feelings are not your problem."

As I listened to Hilda's practical perspective, I began to develop my own realistic answers to the fear thoughts that arose.

Scared Me: What if I get lost?

Realistic Me: Then you'll stop at a gas station and ask for directions.

Scared: But what if I feel foolish?

Realistic: There's no reason to feel foolish. People often need directions if they are not familiar with the area. Service station employees are used to giving directions.

Scared: But what if they see that I'm nervous?

Realistic: They won't notice and, frankly, they don't care. They see hundreds of people come and go each day and they're just thinking about what they'll do at quitting time.

It's very helpful to practice such "realistic" conversations with yourself. When you dissect your fear, you can do some reality checking in a way that isn't possible when your fear is an amorphous, vague apprehension. If you get stumped for an answer to your own questions, you can always fall back on *So what? Who cares?*

The Facts Please, Nothing but the Facts

Whether your fear thoughts are focused on yourself or projected onto other people, getting the facts takes the punch out of anticipating future catastrophes. When my daughter was having her wisdom teeth pulled, I was anxious about her getting anesthesia for the first time and caught myself doing a fear rehearsal. "What if she can't stop bleeding? What if she gets an infection? What if she dies under anesthesia?" I knew I was making myself miserable by dwelling on these catastrophic thoughts, so I called the oral surgeon to do some reality checking. He assured me that out of the 3,018 patients he sees in an average year, he has never had a fatality or a major emergency. He told me that the anesthesia he uses is very light, and the patient continues to breathe completely naturally on her own during the thirty-minute procedure. Once I got the facts, I was able to stop my catastrophic thoughts.

Keep Your Mind Where Your Body Is

We cannot predict the future, nor can we guarantee that we won't have painful challenges. However, when we don't try to get too far ahead of the present moment, we can usually handle what is right in front of us. When I had an irregular Pap smear, I was able to stop my fear rehearsals. Instead of giving up two months of my life imagining what the worst diagnosis might be, I scheduled my follow-up test and chose not to dwell on the subject. Every time my mind drifted to worry, I took a deep breath and said to myself, "I assume I'm fine." In fact, the follow-up test proved I was right.

My brother controlled his anxiety about having surgery by keeping his mind where his body was, at each moment. He discovered that if he broke down the experience to one step at a time, he could handle it. When he registered at the admitting desk, he said to himself, "Fill out these papers? I can handle that." When he changed into a dressing gown, he said to himself, "Change my clothes? I can manage that." When they wheeled him down the corridor, he said to himself, "Lie on this gurney, I can do that." When they administered the anesthesia, he said, "Count backwards from ten? I can handle that." By staying in the present moment with each tangible step, he found out that he could handle everything.

Stimulus Hunting

Edward was afraid to drive on freeways. In order to eliminate this anxiety, he had to identify the specific elements that provoked the fear. This process is called *stimulus hunting*—identifying the specific events and thoughts that trigger the adrenalin. Edward began observing the patterns that characterized his phobia. "I was more comfortable driving at night than in the daytime. I felt safer when it was raining. I felt safer when I wore dark glasses. When I learned about stimulus hunting, I realized the worst scenario for me was driving without sunglasses on a bright sunny day, when my windows were clean, and in gridlock traffic. As I went back over the details, I realized my real fear was that people would see me lose control."

Edward's detective work went from identifying the external stimuli to following the trail of thoughts that led to feelings of humiliation and danger. "In heavy traffic, people have the time to look at me. If they can see me, they're going to know me for who I really am . . . I do not deserve to be at Stanford; the university probably just wanted some Chicanos . . . If my wife really knew me, she'd find out I'm not a loving person . . . I'm somebody who has cheated his way into life and doesn't even deserve to be alive. Mom had two miscarriages before she had me; maybe I should have been a miscarriage."

Edward himself was surprised to discover the avalanche of self-defeating thoughts related to his discomfort at being visible to others. He was able to use his common sense to refute the false beliefs that had become woven into his panic response and to reaffirm the fact that he was intelligent, capable, and deserving of love. Edward continued to work with his self-esteem issues in his phobia support group and his twelve-step A.A. group.

At the same time, he took some tangible, manageable steps directly related to his phobic avoidance pattern. "Stimulus hunting helped me break the problem down, partition it. I could begin by not averting my eyes. In childhood photographs, I tend to look uneasy and face away from the camera, though there are a couple of photos where I'm spontaneous and smiling. I worked my way up to having eye contact with people I knew and later with strangers. When I looked in my wife's eyes, she said she felt warmer about me and more intimate."

Edward learned to recognize and interrupt the chain of subtle, almost unconscious thoughts that triggered his anxiety. "I was especially sensitive to glare or a flash of light. A car in front of me with lots of chrome, or sunlight reflecting off a mirror could trigger uncomfortable sensations. Once I described the thoughts provoked by the glare, I could see how exaggerated they were and change my emotional response. I cleaned my windows and went out driving on a sunny day. I have been able to relax and stop the fear thoughts that made certain ordinary situations seem like a personal threat."

The nervous system normally registers changes in light, activity, or sound. Even when it seems as though you aren't thinking about anything, subtle thoughts arise in association with the external stimuli. Supermarkets, restaurants, and highways provide specific external stimuli such as light, noise, activity, enclosure, open space, unfamiliarity, or distance from home. Associated with these conditions are internal stimuli, which include thoughts and feelings, interpretations of events, and projections of what others are thinking. Your fear thoughts get their power by tapping into memories of past traumas and false beliefs. The danger is not in the bridge, the crowd, or in being alone. It lies in what we tell ourselves that mistakenly links these situations to our core fear of being helpless or hurt.

It is not possible to confront a vague, undefined apprehension, but it is possible to challenge and reevaluate a *specific* external or internal stimulus. By identifying your fear stimuli, you can work with them in small steps. You must be able to distinguish a particular occurrence from an underlying self-defeating belief you may have associated with it. You can use this as an opportunity to explore and perhaps heal old, conditioned patterns that have injured your self-esteem. When a flash of light or an activity in your peripheral vision alarms you, don't mistakenly link your alarm reaction to self-doubts that make you feel inadequate and helpless. The benefit of stimulus hunting is to break down your job of fighting the phobia into more manageable components. It can help you name and confront the false beliefs or self-judging thoughts that fuel your anxiety.

Getting Your Imagination on Your Side

Your rich imagination can be your ally. Claire used relaxation and positive imagery to change her fear rehearsals to success rehearsals. "I relaxed and imagined myself doing something that I thought of as scary. I allowed myself to go through the experience in the safety of lying down in my own bed. For a year, I couldn't ride through a tunnel even with Ray driving. In my visualization, I saw myself riding through a tunnel until the old thoughts came up. 'I can't go through the tunnel because I'll have a panic attack.' I have learned to answer, 'So what, who cares?' and relax my body. I congratulated myself that at least I got to the beginning of the tunnel before I got the panic attack. I went as far as I could before I got anxious, then I would repeat, 'So what?,' relax, and start the visualization all over again. Eventually I was able to stay relaxed while I imagined going through the entire tunnel. After doing the successful rehearsal in my mind, I was able to go through the real tunnel with Ray and stay relaxed." Claire not only practiced switching from tension to relaxation; she also developed a new, more comfortable association with the situation she feared. She was *desensitizing* herself to the idea of riding through the tunnel.

In a similar way, I use visualization to reduce my dread of driving. I imagine myself turning on the ignition, putting on some peaceful classical music and driving onto the freeway. As I approach the bridge, I take a deep, slow breath and note that I feel completely connected to my body—my legs are relaxed; my foot gently touches the brake to slow down, then moves back to the accelerator to keep up with the flow of traffic. On my right I see the blue water of the bay framed by the profile of downtown buildings. The minute I notice a fear thought or an increase in muscle tension, I relax and calm myself by imagining my "special place" under a tree in the country. I wait for my body to relax completely, then return to the image of driving once again. I envision easily maneuvering the car into the middle lane. I conclude by arriving at my destination in plenty of time, greeted by the hug of my friend, who is so happy to see me. Each time I practice the scene in my mind, my body feels more comfortable. In this way, I approach the things I have avoided, while still sitting in my armchair. The *thought* of driving on the bridge does not trigger adrenalin anymore.

Fightin' Words

Kathy was determined to get her life back, even though she had to move painstakingly slow. She learned to talk realistically to herself, citing her record of successes rather than the potential for failure. "Sometimes after I started working in the front yard again, I'd get tense and think, 'It's starting to happen,' and I'd want to flee and get in the house where no one could see me lose control. Then I would say to myself, 'For God's sake, you've been doing this now for *weeks*. Knock it off! You can do it, you've already been doing it!' There have

been times when I just had to say, 'Oh screw it, *do* it!'"
Getting tough with the phobia helps Kathy move forward even when fear thoughts arise.

I too have discovered that being assertive with my
phobia reduces anxiety. My body feels different when I
use the language of strength and determination. This is
not something I could do in the beginning, but once I
had some victories over the phobia, I realized that I
was stronger than the Phoboo. Driving across the
bridge, I used my fightin' words to combat fear
thoughts. "I have a life to live, and you can't stop me.
Get out of my way. I have places to go and people to
see." I call those my fightin' words because they make
me feel like a warrior. They seem to change my body
chemistry too. "You're not gonna run my life! I've done
this before and I can do it again." You can have a conversation with your phobia, either by talking or writing
to it. Get tough with it. You have a life to live that's too
important to let your phobia take the reins.

Fear is a valuable reflex that is meant to warn you
of danger. The kind of fear thoughts that lead you to
panic, however, are not based on real threats or real
facts. Your style of thinking and even the content of
your thoughts is as much of a learned habit as how you
walk or hold your pen. The majority of things we fear
never actually happen to us. Those things that do happen are part of our life journey, and as sensitive, intelligent, resourceful people, we usually find a way to handle the real crises. Don't wear yourself out handling the
imaginary ones. Howard pushed back the Phoboo by
depriving it of fear juice; Claire faced the sensations
and disarmed the threat of panic; Kathy used fightin'

words to push aside her fear thoughts. You can experiment with different thought-stopping and thought-changing techniques and decide which ones work best for you. *You can change the way you think.*

How About You?

1. Naming Fear Thoughts

For one day, track your thoughts. In your journal, write down your fear thoughts, paying special attention to exactly what you were thinking before you started to get anxious. Include the What Ifs and the WPTs.

Read over your entries and underline the words that make you nervous.

2. "So What?" Confront Your Fear Thoughts

Set aside a specific time period to practice stopping your fear thoughts. Choose one thought-stopping technique from this chapter and use it every single time you have a fear thought or a thought that undermines your self-esteem or confidence. Write down a fact that disputes your fear thoughts, answer them with realistic thinking or use your favorite fear stopper ("So what? Who cares?"). Can you take the punch out of them? Write down the results in your journal.

3. Stimulus Hunting

Choose one fear thought from the exercise and write it down in your journal. Briefly, picture the situation described by that thought and list the external stimuli that affect you, such as sights, sounds, conditions. Then write about the thoughts that relate to the situation, such as, "What if I run into people I know and they see I'm nervous?"

When you peel away the layers of your thoughts to reveal the core, you'll begin to discover that it's not the situation, it's your thoughts or interpretation of the situation that scare you. Then you will be ready to stop and change these fear-provoking thoughts. In some cases, you may need additional guidance to help you decide whether your concerns, especially the WPTs, are realistic or imagined.

7

An Inch Is a Cinch: Gradual Exposure

To beat your phobias, you must return to the situations you have avoided, equipped with skills and choices. Every step you take is a victory, and with every victory you reclaim territory from the Phoboo. But the Phoboo is a stubborn creature who has a stake in keeping you scared. "Just because you walked alone once doesn't mean you can do it again," he taunts. "You can drive when the highway is empty, but what if there's traffic?" The best antidote to his litany of fear and doubt is practice, practice, practice. With thought stopping and relaxation, you can stand your ground and multiply your successes. When you've done something ten or twenty times, you can answer with certainty, "I've done it before and I can do it again. What If thoughts can't stop me anymore!" To overcome a phobia, you must accumulate enough victories to vanquish the Phoboo.

A Step-by-Step Hierarchy

The purpose of gradually exposing yourself to the situations you have avoided is not just to reach a goal, but to do it in a way that gives you the experience of being calm and confident. This approach is different from the old coping skill of "white-knuckling" your way through your fear and then hoping you'll never have to fly or drive or shop again. When you learn to face your fear with a system that allows you to move at your own pace, you'll *want* to return again.

Working with Hilda, I learned how to desensitize myself to each phobic fear. First I set an objective, such as driving down a steep hill. (San Francisco is very accommodating for confronting this fear!) Then we outlined a sequential plan of activities called a *desensitization hierarchy.* This hierarchy can be pictured as a ladder, the bottom rung representing the easiest step, the top rung representing the final goal. Each step up represents an increasingly challenging action. The value of a hierarchy is that it provides a gently paced system for approaching intimidating situations and finding out that your thought-changing and relaxation tools *do* work.

Often the first step in a hierarchy can be as simple as cutting out pictures that represent the situation you are working on. I used a newspaper clipping of cars driving down Lombard Street, famous for being the steepest, most winding street in San Francisco. I began to desensitize myself to the thought of driving down the hill by looking at the picture, relaxing, and looking at it again until the image evoked no reaction. Then I taped it on my refrigerator and looked at it so often that it stopped having special significance.

A hierarchy provides a flexible working structure that can be adjusted to match your experience. You can repeat any step over and over until you feel confident about it; you can add more intermediate steps if you find that you need them, or you may skip steps if you discover you don't need them. Often just spending more time in a situation or progressing from doing it with a support person to being able to do it on your own provides the momentum you need to reach your goal.

The Five R's

Hilda also introduced me to a set of guidelines developed by the TERRAP treatment program, called the five Rs: *React—Retreat—Relax—Return—Repeat*. These stages can be used to master each step on your hierarchy. To show me how they worked, Hilda got in the car with me and drove to the top of a very steep hill. I gasped (*React*) and blurted out, "I'm not ready." Without hesitation, she took a right turn (*Retreat*) and drove for three or four minutes on level ground. "Do your deep, slow breathing" (*Relax*), she reminded me. "Bring yourself back down to zero anxiety just as when you practice in your armchair." Once I stopped my fearful thoughts and calmed myself, I felt ready to go down the hill (*Return*). Breathing very slowly and deeply, I stayed below a level one on the anxiety scale for the whole ride. After we had gone down three times (*Repeat*), I was ready to go on to the next step in my hierarchy and do the driving myself.

In subsequent months, I used the same system for approaching elevators, freeways, bridges, and tunnels, sometimes practicing with a companion, at other times going out on my own. Just knowing *how* to practice, and having choices, made me more willing to take new risks. Over time I learned that if I remained in the situation and didn't add frightening or catastrophic thoughts, the anxiety symptoms would subside naturally. I knew that I could physically retreat if I chose to, or mentally retreat by changing my thoughts or imagining my "special place." Even when I did physically withdraw from a situation, I knew it was my belief that I would feel better rather than the actual change of location that lowered my anxiety.

The More I Practice, the Luckier I Get

As I accomplished each step, I moved further along my hierarchy of actions. Yet I was still attached to some of my old patterns. I wanted to stay in the right lane, my "safe" lane. I wanted to take my "familiar" on-ramp. I wanted to travel the same route, or drive at a speed slower than the rest of the traffic. Hilda would smile at me in her kind way and say, "Mani, that's phobic thinking. A road is a road; driving is the same everywhere—four wheels on the road. What's the difference between one road and another? You don't need to know everything in advance. You can handle what comes up. *You are your own safe person. Wherever you are is your safe place.*"

After I drove with Hilda past four exits on an unfamiliar freeway, she told me, "You've got it, Mani. Before returning home, go back and forth three or four more times by yourself." "But Hilda, doesn't this count as a victory?" I asked. "It sure does," she agreed, "and every victory means you are getting your life back. Now go out and do it again and again, until it's just ordinary."

I discovered that I had to repeat the actions soon after my sessions with Hilda, preferably the same day or the next day, even if I went a shorter distance. If I let too much time go by, I started to dread driving again. I had to remind myself: "I am the one who drove down the freeway. *My* hands were on the steering wheel. *My* foot was on the brake. If I did it once, I can do it again!"

One day during my solo practice time, I drove on the freeway beyond my planned stopping point. I felt so exhilarated that I went another five miles and pulled into a shopping mall. I bought myself a pair of pants covered with violet flowers and some high-top tennis shoes I had wanted for a long time. Every time I wore my new clothes, I remembered how confident and strong I had felt that day driving on the highway. I had discovered the sixth R— *Reward*. Whether you buy yourself a present, treat yourself to a massage, or congratulate yourself with a good pat on the back, your reward is a tangible reminder that you are regaining ground. Your "brain in a bag" is impressed by rewards and begins to believe that you can do it.

Boredom Can Be a Sign of Success

Edward's technique was to do each step of his hierarchy until he was bored with it. "For me, boredom was a good alternative to anxiety. I would sit in the car with the engine off until I started daydreaming. That meant

I had achieved boredom. Then I did the same thing with the engine running. When my mind started wandering to other things in my life, my anxiety disappeared. Later I would drive to the foot of a short bridge and look at it until I was absolutely bored. That might take forty-five minutes. I would get so bored I would even look forward to the next step of driving on the bridge." Because boredom is devoid of excitement or anxiety, it does not stimulate added adrenalin and can produce a physiological state similar to feeling calm. Naturally, daydreaming does not work as a relaxation method if you fill your mind with fearful thoughts, but if you keep your focus on the present situation, boredom can become a positive association.

How long do you need to practice? How often? How much is enough? You'll know it's enough when you don't dread or find excuses to avoid. Edward's instructor gave him a card that said, *"The sooner fear is faced, the better. The longer fear is faced, the better."* His program recommended that he practice for at least two hours twice a week. Edward did this so deliberately that one day a police officer stopped him to question why he kept driving back and forth on the main street. Edward explained that he was phobic and was just practicing his driving. The officer respected his explanation.

Every Tiny Step Counts

After being homebound for so long, Kathy's first challenge was to spend some time outside her house. During her third weekly phone appointment with Dr. Liebgold, he suggested that she write up a hierarchy using the gardening work that she had once loved. He assured her that she was under no time pressure and needed only to report whatever she experienced each week.

At first Kathy became anxious just thinking about being outside working in the garden. "It was too scary to think of the whole picture. But I told myself, 'I'll try this for a few minutes, and if I feel okay, I can stay longer.' Every step was on a minimal scale, and I'd add a couple of minutes at a time." Kathy's first major goal was to work outside for two hours. Her ten-step hierarchy was very specific:

1. Go out to the front yard and sit on the porch for two minutes.
2. Sit on porch for five minutes (keep adding time).
3. Water lawn in the morning when few people are on street.
4. Water lawn in the afternoon when more people are around.
5. Pick weeds for two minutes in the morning (keep adding time).
6. Pick weeds for two minutes in the afternoon (keep adding time).
7. Mow one strip of lawn.
8. Mow two strips of lawn.
9. Mow half the lawn.
10. Work outside for two hours. Trim the driveway, mow the whole lawn, weed, and water.

According to Kathy, "At first it was a major ordeal to sit out there. I worried that someone would come down the street and see me. What if they looked at me and knew something was wrong? When I let myself dwell on those fearful What If thoughts, I would get dizzy from the adrenalin and have to go back in. I felt safer if I stayed right by the door or if I was near a tree that I could hide behind."

Kathy was relieved to have something specific to do each day and someone to discuss it with. "The first week I wanted someone to be out there with me, but soon I started going out by myself. If I became too uncomfortable, I came back into the house, took some time to calm down, and then went back out again." After about a week, she realized that nobody was really looking at her. She mowed one strip of grass, then returned and did two. The following day she mowed half the lawn.

Kathy made her hierarchy a priority and gave herself credit for her victories, knowing every achievement counted, no matter how small. She accomplished her first goal faster than she thought she would. "After three weeks I was able to go outside by myself and do the whole job. I weeded the front lawn, mowed and trimmed it, swept and washed down the driveway, and sat out there feeling like a million dollars."

Kathy saw that the system of gradually exposing herself to her feared situations worked. Her next objective was to go out to public places again. By then she was able to enlist Trina's help to expand her territory.

"When I started going to stores, I took it in baby steps. At first I could only get in the car with Trina and ride to the parking lot. I had to take a deep breath and tell myself 'You can do this.' The next step was to walk from the parking lot to the store. In the beginning I chose little stores, located very close to the parking lot, with easy access to the exit. Later on I went into larger stores."

In order to stay in stores for any length of time, Kathy had to become very conscious of her body posture. "I had to be aware if my knees were locked and remember to stand in a looser way. I had to breathe slowly and tell myself, 'You only need to stay a few minutes.' Later on I discovered that I could calm myself by putting my mind on other things. It had been so long since I had been in a store that I was fascinated by all the new items on the shelves and forgot my fear for longer periods of time. Little things that seemed insignificant to other people were huge for me. Each tiny step was big. When I put all these tiny things together, I began to see the entire picture. *When I measured my progress, not in days, but in months, I could hardly believe what I had mastered.*"

For almost a year, Trina accompanied Kathy to stores, to doctors' appointments, and to do errands. Sometimes Kathy felt exhilarated after an outing, and other times she felt exhausted. Afterward, they spent long hours together talking. Trina recalled how excited she herself used to get during her early days of mastering new situations. Even though she shared Kathy's enthusiasm every time she accomplished a new goal, Trina would often remind her, "Okay, dear heart, this has been a three-hour marathon. Now you'd better take a rest before you do anything else." Whatever happened, Trina always congratulated Kathy for what she had accomplished. Kathy relied on the practical and emotional support of her friend.

One day, Kathy took a new risk. She rarely went anywhere with her husband, whose impatience heightened her anxiety. But Kathy was feeling confident from her recent successes, so she drove with him to the pet store and went in by herself to buy some dog food. She was very excited and eager to share her victory with Trina, but decided to wait until after the weekend because she knew Trina had house guests. On Sunday she got a call from Trina's aunt who told her that Trina had suffered a stroke and died. The news was devastating for Kathy.

"I felt heartsick when I heard that Trina died. She was so young and such a caring person. And she was my lifeline and I didn't know how I would go on without her. It took some time to learn to trust myself again and to remember that I was okay. I had to force myself to get up in the morning. But I did, and sometimes I felt as though she was here with me, like my guardian angel. I could hear her voice saying, 'Kathy, you're going to have to go on and take chances, dear heart.'"

Kathy was deeply grieved by her friend's death, but she turned her love for her friend into the courage to go on. She learned to ask for help from other people, including her sister, her daughter, and, gradually, other friends. She continued to read her phobia workbook, plan new hierarchies, and call Dr. Liebgold to report her progress.

Getting There with a Success Rehearsal

The best incentive to work on a hierarchy is to set a goal that really matters to you. Kathy was highly motivated by a desire to go to her daughter's graduation.

"She is so special to me, and this was her big day. I also thought, 'Trina can't be there to see her daughter graduate, but I am more fortunate. I can be there if I make up my mind to do it.'"

So Kathy used her mind to prepare for the graduation. In her imagination, she created a *success rehearsal*, going over every part of the day in detail. "I had been to the stadium before and could picture the setting. Over and over during the preceding weeks, I mentally visualized arriving at the parking lot in plenty of time so I could move slowly. Next, I pictured myself walking slowly with my family into the stadium, feeling happy and relaxed. I saw myself going to a row of seats right near the exit of the stadium so I could leave if I needed to. I planned it out and lived it through many times in my mind, relaxing my body as I pictured everything happening calmly and smoothly.

"Graduation day was sunny and hot. I kept the car keys in my hand so I could go back to the car at any time. My mother and sister sat with me in the shaded area I had chosen near the exit. My husband and cousins sat closer to the stage so they could take pictures. I was so motivated to stay that even when I got nervous, I used my tools and told myself I could do it. Being there meant so much to me. I was really proud of myself for sitting through the whole ceremony."

You can work on your desensitization hierarchy by doing a success rehearsal of each step on your list. This is also called a *mental hierarchy.* You visualize each activity unfolding in a calm and reassuring way. If at any point on your mental hierarchy you become anxious, use your thought-changing and relaxation skills to return to a level zero on the anxiety scale, then go back to the scene in your imagination and move through it step by step.

It takes faith to remember that all these little steps are going to add up to having choices that create more freedom in your life. Kathy found out that every victory strengthened her trust in herself and in her ability to effectively use her anxiety-reducing skills. As she breathed more easily, she began to remember what it was like to have things that she cared about in her life. A few weeks after the graduation, still delighting in her victory, Kathy went to the phobia class for the first time and finally met Dr. Liebgold in person.

Support That Helps You Become Independent

Many of us who have been phobic are already dependent on other people for practical help. In planning a desensitization process, it is essential to find a balance between the support received from others and the reliance on your own ability to take care of yourself. If you are enlisting other people for support, be sure you also include actions in your hierarchy that you can do entirely by yourself. Although it is very important to get help at certain stages, it is misleading to think that the other person makes you safe. What always makes you safe is your knowledge of what is happening in your body, your ability to think realistically rather than catastrophically, and your consistent use of relaxation and stress-reduction skills.

For example, having Hilda accompany me in the car served some specific functions. She was available to help me pinpoint and change my unrealistic and phobic thinking patterns. She provided emotional comfort to the part of me that wasn't willing to take risks without a hand to hold. Her confidence in me helped me believe in myself. But once she had supported me in these ways, she made it very clear that I had done the work and had proof that my new skills would work. Now I needed to put my trust in myself.

A support person does not need to have professional training or special expertise. Those of us with anxiety need someone who respects our learning process, is not frightened by our feelings, and is willing to respond in the ways we request. Sometimes what we ask for takes time and effort: "Will you drive with me to the city to do some Christmas shopping?" At other times, our request is more simple: "Can I call you to check in just before I leave?" The most important thing is to know what we need and to explain our request clearly to the other person.

Kathy wanted to buy a new stove and asked for help from a friend with whom she hadn't gone out since her panic attacks began. "I told her ahead of time, 'If I need to leave, I want to leave immediately, no questions asked.'" Her friend left the car door unlocked so Kathy could get in the car fast if she needed to. Knowing that she had set up a safety net for herself, Kathy was able to go to two stores, return home to measure the area in the kitchen, and go back and buy the stove. "I paid for it and talked to the salesman, all at level zero. I was astounded at my composure, and pleased with myself."

It's Great to Have Phobic Friends

People who have experienced panic or have phobias can be a great support to each other. Our common experiences give us compassion and respect for each other; yet having different issues allows us to be helpful and at ease in a situation that someone else may consider difficult.

I became friends with a woman I met in the first phobia group I attended. Sometimes after class, I followed her car on the freeway, finding the courage to start driving at night by bonding with her friendly taillights. One day she asked me to help her ride the local commuter train. My friend had already overcome many fears but was still struggling with being in trains and airplanes. "Riding in the train is a step toward flying, which is my big goal," she told me. "Being on a train brings up the same fear of being trapped and unable to get off."

On the appointed day, she met me at the station and we went up the escalator to the passenger platform. She was nervous, but used the controlled deep breathing she had learned in class. When the train pulled up, she bravely entered the car and sat down by the window seat. She kept her attention on the physical things around her—the signs, the textures, the colors.

It turned out to be an uneven train ride. The train stopped several times between stations and then continued slowly with jerks and starts until it got to the next station. In spite of an increase in anxiety, my friend used her deep breathing to stay composed.

We exited the train and, after complimenting her on how well she had handled the situation, I asked her what she wanted to do next. We had previously agreed that she was in charge and always had the option of getting off the train. Uncertain for a moment, she looked at me sheepishly and said, "We could take a cab back." "Oh dear," I said, "I don't really like riding in a cab with a driver who doesn't understand my phobia." We looked at each other and started to laugh. We laughed so hard that tears rolled down our cheeks. "You don't like the train and I don't like a cab. We're a great team!" The truth is, we *were* a great team. We felt better after laughing at our predicament, and we were both willing to use our calming breathing and talk ourselves through whatever option we chose.

The next train pulled into the station and my friend decided to get on. Although the outside conditions were not ideal, she had a victory that day, one that paved the way to taking her next step. I didn't see her very much after our group ended, but I got a call from her about a year later telling me she had just *flown* back from a vacation in New Orleans. She was elated!

Inch by Inch

Claire's life had become increasingly restricted during the year she underwent so many medical tests. She was eager to become active again, and discovered that the process of moving through her hierarchies was fun. Going to the supermarket alone was her first big goal.

"I realized I had been avoiding even looking at stores when out doing errands with my husband. So I started by just observing the front of a store. After a while I became comfortable having a store in my vision. Next, I would touch the store. I am very tactile, and the more I can use all my senses, the better for me. I'd feel the tile on the outside wall and eventually make friends with the store. Sometimes I felt ridiculous, but one of my most important tools while practicing was being gentle with myself and celebrating that I was taking care of myself by doing whatever I could.

"The first few steps on my hierarchy were pretty easy, but the big challenge was going up to the front door. My thoughts about the automatic door scared me: 'Once you go in, you're trapped; what if the doors don't open and you have to break the glass to get out?' Pretty catastrophic stories! So I would go up to the door, step on the mat, watch the door open, and walk away. Inch by inch, I got myself into the store, always giving myself permission to leave at any time and always making a promise to myself that if I left, I would come back later."

Initially, Claire relied on distraction techniques to master each step, but once in the store, she discovered something that worked even better for her. "When you first walk into the grocery store, you see all these beautiful fruits and you can go up and smell them. I found myself picking up and smelling the fruits and vegetables, and being right there with them. It was so wonderful because when I'm in the present moment, there's no room for panic. Panic can only find me if I am off into the future and the What If thoughts."

When Claire first learned to use a hierarchy, she relied entirely on her husband, Ray, to go with her to practice. She soon became frustrated "because I wanted to practice all the time and we couldn't always coordinate our schedules. After I understood that it wasn't the store, it wasn't the elevator, it wasn't the tunnel—it was about knowing what was going on in me and taking care of me—then I realized I didn't need to be with Ray to practice.

"I remember the first time I went on an elevator without Ray. I was walking with a colleague, and as we headed toward the elevators, I found myself thinking, 'Oh, I can practice walking up to an elevator, and when she gets in, I'll take the stairs.' When we got to the elevator and she walked in, I realized I wanted to be in that elevator too! I put my hands on the inside of the doors and I said to her, 'Dierdre, I have had panic attacks and I'm not comfortable with elevators. In fact, they terrify me. But I would really like to get into this elevator right now and ride up with you. I needed you to know that before I try.'

"She was wonderful. She reached out her hand toward me and invited me in. I thought I was only going to stay on for one floor, but we rode up three. We got off the elevator and she gave me the biggest hug. Unexpectedly I had found myself with an opportunity and, rather than looking at it as an opportunity to panic, it became a chance to practice.

"When I first heard *practice,* it sounded like something I *had* to do, like brushing my teeth. I didn't put working on my hierarchy in the same category as the joy of driving on the highway to pick up my wonderful eight-year-old niece, and spending the day playing with her. But I discovered that practicing isn't separate from life. Practicing is living my life, every minute."

"I Can Handle It"

When we first start working on our hierarchies, we want to know everything in advance—what to expect, who will be there, where we will be sitting, how we can leave. When we don't believe that we have control over our own bodies (sensations) and over our own thoughts (fear thoughts), we think we will feel safer if we have control over outside conditions—the traffic, the weather, the behavior of other people. In the beginning of our desensitization, we set up conditions that will give us this external control. We leave the door open, drive in the right lane, shop in small stores, sit in the aisle seat. Having an escape plan, a retreat option, an antianxiety drug, or a support person, can restore our shaken confidence. This is a very important phase of our process, but it is not our ultimate goal. Practicing our phobia-healing skills, we begin to renew our trust in our ability to take care of ourselves, even if events don't unfold exactly as we had anticipated.

Howard was relentless in pursuing his hierarchies. He mastered sitting in the middle seat in a theater, then went on to test his freedom to come and go as he pleased. In sports stadiums he took an inside seat and then threw his keys under the bleachers so he had to say, "Excuse me," to twenty people as he stepped over them to get out in the middle of a game to retrieve his keys. He assured himself that not only could he use his relaxation and thought-changing tools to stay calm, but also that he would never again let the WPTs inhibit his choices.

The desensitization process worked so well that he used the same system to confront his fear of feeling trapped on public conveyances such as buses and underground trains. "After two shorter practice rides, I was able to get on the train and go all the way through the tunnel at a level two. On the way back, my anxiety level was between zero and one half. After making the same trip several more times, I felt satisfied that I really had taken care of my phobia about confinement in public transportation."

Six months later, Howard got to use the tickets that had once precipitated a fear rehearsal. "I took my son to the Olympic Games and sat with one hundred twenty-five thousand people. I had tears in my eyes because it was a very moving, patriotic ceremony and because I sat there with zero anxiety. The next morning I went out to jog and discovered that my car had been stolen. I was wondering how we were going to get home. Then I thought, 'Wow, this is a great opportunity! I can handle it!' We booked a plane flight, then took the commuter train home from the airport. I did the whole thing with no anxiety."

Working through a desensitization hierarchy takes time and patience. Sometimes we feel resistant to working on an objective that doesn't satisfy our immediate needs. But by mastering the situations that trigger anxiety, we begin to dissolve the artificial delineation between "safe" and "unsafe." Howard rarely depended on public transportation, and could afford any seat he wanted in a theater. But after living a restricted life for thirty-one years, he wasn't willing to settle for choices based on artificial considerations. The minute he identified any area that triggered his phobic feelings, he immediately set up a hierarchy and got to work on it.

Building on Your Victories

The two months Alicia spent working as an intern in a city office had been challenging for her. Yet, to her surprise, the feeling of triumph she experienced by staying with it and reaching her goals began to affect the way she felt about the rest of her life. She noticed that other situations she had once dreaded were becoming easier. "When my daughter graduated from college, I went to a dinner with the families of her friends and sat at a table with people I hadn't met before. As I socialized with them, I felt relaxed because eating gave me something to do. Every now and then I realized, 'I'm doing okay,' and patted myself on the back for it. When I got home, I thought, 'I was just a regular person today!' And the nice part was that I enjoyed myself."

A few weeks later, Alicia went to the local college to look into taking some classes. "Even thinking of going back to school had seemed like an insurmountable step a few years ago. But I was feeling so much better about myself and I wanted to learn more about the things that interest me. I found a program in consulting psychology with an emphasis on holistic health. I believe that so much of our mental attitude is determined by our physical well-being—what we eat and how we use our bodies. I thought this program sounded perfect for me." Alicia began to get excited about new possibilities that involved helping others, such as teaching or setting up holistic programs for people with panic disorders. Her desire to participate in something meaningful to her became such a strong motivation that it helped her get through her anxiety.

Alicia enrolled in two night classes. The day of her first class she felt some dread, but she used thought-stopping and realistic thinking. "I said to myself, 'STOP! This is just in your head. It takes everyone a while to get to know other people.' And remembering my experience working in the city office, I added, 'I know I'll feel more at ease as time goes by.'"

Moving Through Disappointments

Alicia had a few uneasy moments during her first weeks at school, but, considering that it had been almost twenty years since she'd been a student, she acknowledged she was doing very well. Then, in her second semester, she started to feel agitated in her Tuesday night class. She practiced her slow diaphragmatic breathing, but it took all her concentration to sit through the evening. The following week, she was apprehensive and felt even more uncomfortable. Once again she used her skills and stayed for the whole class.

Alicia was surprised by her reaction because she had been so confident the first semester. When she examined her life, she realized that within a short time she had sold her house, moved, and made a sizable commitment to a program that included self-exploration as well as educational instruction. She recognized that in her excitement at getting so much better, she had taken on too many commitments. She decided to reduce the pressure she had put on herself and dropped some less important plans. But her discomfort continued. "I began to feel restricted again and was afraid my world would start shrinking. What I was doing meant too much to me to retreat. I did not want to drop out of the program."

Alicia used the temporary setback to reassess her situation and modify her healing plan. "Unlike in the past when I just quit because I had no information or tools, I decided to consider all my choices." She was able to see her discomfort as part of a larger process of growth.

Alicia made an appointment with a psychiatrist who specialized in medication for anxiety. She tried a few different options, and found that a low dose of an antidepressant made enough difference that she didn't dwell on anxiety or add alarming thoughts even if some physical symptoms occurred. "If I felt anxiety, I just said to myself, 'Okay, I'm going to acknowledge it, say good-bye to it, and wish it on its way.' That got me to relax."

She also asked for support from her instructor. "We had an all-day seminar coming up, so I called up the teacher to tell her what was going on. She asked me, 'How can I make it safe for you to be there?' I could tell that she was willing to support me so I could stay in the class. I asked her to describe what we were going to do for the day, and she gave me a brief outline of her plan. Several times during the seminar, she said, 'If someone doesn't want to do this or needs to take a break and go outside, go ahead.' That made me feel that my needs were being considered. I also used the exercise, 'Breathing in, I relax my body. Breathing out, I smile.' At the end of the day, I looked at the teacher and raised my fist in the air as a victory sign. I'm so glad I talked to her. It made all the difference in the world. I came home and felt on top of the world because I got through the class."

Alicia felt good about taking care of herself in this way and was glad that she didn't let a setback stop her. She was able to participate in every class project and complete the semester with renewed enthusiasm for her courses.

A Realistic Attitude Toward Setbacks

Living a totally anxiety-free life is not a realistic goal. Being realistic means trusting that you have reliable tools to handle whatever comes up, and knowing that as uncomfortable as you may feel, you won't die. Sometimes our disappointments even provide us with a new piece of information or lead us to a missing step. They give us a chance to reevaluate our course and to develop a more kind and compassionate attitude toward ourselves. Even if we need to slow down or temporarily go back to an earlier step, our overall progress continues. Edward describes disappointments as similar to temporary static on a TV screen. "If I just go back to relaxation and take whatever step is possible, the program gets back into focus and I go on with my life."

"I don't even use the word *setback*," Claire told me, "because it has a connotation that something must be wrong. We all have different learning rates and a lot of things come into play. For me it is never really a step back, because I am never where I used to be. I have all this experience to draw upon. I feel like I am always moving forward in a circular kind of way."

Remember that progress in anything we do—our careers, our relationships, creative projects—is rarely a straight line. Usually we experience a series of peaks and valleys which, when viewed over a long period, show a larger pattern of progress. By using our tools and good judgment, we can include these ups and downs as a natural part of our healing process.

Keeping a Victory Log

One way to focus on your progress is to keep a *Victory Log* in which you record the date and content of each accomplishment. No matter how small, each one counts! To stay motivated, you need to give yourself credit for every action and let your successes speak louder than your disappointments.

When I was working on driving across the bridge, I thought it would be fun to make a collage victory chart to record my success. I covered a piece of poster board with colored paper and pasted on it postcards of the Bay Bridge. Then I made a game of collecting the toll slips. Each time I paid my dollar at the toll booth, I asked the toll taker for my "reward." When I got home I stapled the toll slip to the collage and embellished it with gold stars and Garfield stickers that said "Yes, you can!" "You are great!" and "Way to go!" At the end of two months, I had nineteen toll slips and a convincing reminder that each one represented the victory of my hands firmly in charge at the steering wheel.

Kathy uses her kitchen calendar as a victory log to record her increasing range of activity. "I try to put something on my calendar every day. I don't go into detail, but if I was able to stay calm and enjoy myself, I put a circle with a smiling face next to the entry. As my calendar gets full, it reminds me of how far I've come." Kathy's calendar works because it is always visible and gives her motivation to do more each day.

Climbing the Eiffel Tower

One night I had a dream that showed me that my beliefs about what I could do were changing on a deep level. In the dream, I am in a class in which people are dancing in a circle around a high tower. A woman comes into the class and says to the teacher, "I can't climb up that tower." I look up and see a very tall metal structure similar to the Eiffel Tower. I think to myself, "I can't climb it either because I might get panicky feelings when I get up high." Then I remember, "Wait a minute, if I go just one little step at a time, I'll be fine. I don't have to rush myself. If each day I just go one step higher, I'll grow accustomed to that step." At that moment in the dream, I had the experience of *knowing* that I can do it.

As you master more and more of the situations that used to frighten you, you will be able to operate with a spontaneity that you could not even have imagined. Kathy recalled, "One night I got the urge to take my dog, Cody, for a walk. It was ten o'clock on a beautiful summer night, and my husband was at the store. I grabbed Cody's leash and walked out the door. I quit thinking and just did it. I feel so much more like *me* as I get my impulsiveness back."

When you take a single step followed by another, inch by inch, mile by mile, you are on your way to reclaiming your life again. Moving along your hierarchy with patient determination takes you beyond the ability to go shopping or drive or attend classes. It gives you back the freedom to be yourself.

How About You?

1. Plan a Hierarchy

On an empty page in your journal, draw a ladder. Number the steps from one to ten, beginning with the bottom rung. Choose a goal that is important to you and write it next to the number ten at the top of page. Determine an action you could do now, no matter how small, and write it at the bottom of the page, next to number one. Now fill in steps two through nine in pencil (so you can change them if needed), increasing the time, the distance, or the challenge on each step. Applaud yourself for being creative in facing your fear and allow yourself to include steps that may be beyond your expectations at this moment.

10. **GOAL: Birthday dinner with friends at Chez Panisse**
 9. Have dinner with friends at medium-size restaurant
 8. Have early-bird dinner with friends at small restaurant
 7. Go to coffee shop and have lunch with two friends
 6. Go to coffee shop with a friend and order lunch
 5. Go to fast-food place and have a Coke with a friend
 4. Go to fast-food place and have a drink and side order there
 3. Go to fast-food place and order a Coke to go
 2. Go into small restaurant, look around, and leave
 1. Look at picture of people dining out

2. Practice a Mental Hierarchy

Sit in a comfortable chair and take a few minutes to breathe deeply and relax your body. Now imagine each of the actions in your hierarchy, going systematically from step one to step ten. If at any point your anxiety starts to rise or you begin to do a fear rehearsal, STOP immediately, open your eyes, and remind yourself of your present reality. Touch the fabric of the chair, look around. Use your deep, slow breathing and relaxation skills to return to a level zero, and then begin the visualization again. Go as far as you can each day until you have a successful mental rehearsal.

3. Do It!

Do one step on your hierarchy. When you're able to accomplish step one while staying low on the anxiety scale, go on to step two. You can repeat the same step as often as you need to until you feel you've mastered it. Reward yourself for each practice. Say positive things to yourself, buy yourself a present, give yourself a gold star. If any step requires assistance, ask for help.

4. Make a Victory Chart

Choose a section in your journal and write "My Victories" at the top of the page. Each time you accomplish a step on your hierarchy, record the date and the action on your chart. Use stars or stickers to highlight your entries. Or, write all your victories on a monthly calendar that you keep in a prominent place. You will get a good perspective on how much you are doing and a great sense of accomplishment from seeing this. For example:

My Victories

2/21 Spoke in my small conference group ★
2/25 Stood up in class and read a one-page report ★

8

Respecting Your Own Voice

As you change your response to specific territorial and social situations, you may find that you have a greater incentive to respect your own voice in *all* the interactions in your life. When words or feelings are stifled, they remain in our bodies as tension or pain; sometimes they feel bottled-up, like a volcano threatening to erupt. When we try to hide something, we may develop a heightened concern that other people can see through us and discover our secrets. To avoid conflict or to accommodate the expectations of others, we "tie ourselves in knots" or "bend over backward." These metaphors reflect the mental and physical stress we endure based on our belief that we must manage our relationships at the expense of our emotional freedom and self-expression.

We are appalled at our fear of losing control on the highway. We worry about someone seeing us tremble in the supermarket checkout line. But these situations may be reflections of a deeper fear of not being able to manage an accumulation of unexpressed feelings. The journey of recovering from panic and phobias often compels us to reevaluate the emotional defenses we have adopted to protect ourselves from being hurt. In the process of healing, we find renewed respect for our own voice.

Recovering Feelings

As Bonnie gained confidence in using her skills to reduce anxiety, she recognized the emotional patterns that had contributed to her tension and to her feelings of being trapped. "I realized I had to educate myself not only about the specifics of phobias, but also about the related emotional issues. I had never learned a constructive way to deal with feelings of anger or jealousy, or with my fear of rejection. I didn't even know how to recognize or express my emotions because as a child I had learned to suppress them. If I was upset about something, I would shut down and withdraw into a resentful silence. When I cut off the unpleasant feelings, I shut off the pleasant ones as well. It became increasingly clear to me that I needed to make changes in my life that included expressing anger and asserting myself."

Bonnie again turned to the psychology section of her local library. She picked out a book that focused on anger, as well as some inspirational self-help books. They gave her a new perspective on the importance of identifying different feelings as well as examples of the kind of language she could use to express herself in a healthy way. "It took a concerted effort, but gradually I began to rediscover and express my feelings. I had to face the fear that I would be rejected as I had been in the past, when a friend stopped talking to me after a disagreement. At the time I felt hurt and abandoned and blamed myself. As I was learning the importance of expressing my feelings, I developed a new friendship with a woman who was willing to listen to me and discuss differences. She didn't get upset and drop me if I told her that something bothered me. That was a tremendous help, and gave me confidence in my ability to voice my feelings."

Her familiar concerns about being hurt or rejected still came up, but Bonnie understood more clearly how holding back her feelings had added to her anxiety. "Not expressing those feelings and not speaking up for myself brought on the panic disorder as a kind of delayed reaction. I let all that tension build up inside of me. My panic attacks were my body's way of demanding my attention and saying, 'I'm going to *make* you listen to your feelings.' When I began recovering my feelings and expressing them, my general anxiety level decreased. Now if I get in the car and start to feel anxious, I say to myself, 'What's going on for you? Are you holding something in? Is something causing you anger or frustration?' When I realize that my feelings are hurt or that I am angry, I go back to my husband or my stepmother or my friend and say, 'There is something I didn't say earlier. I want to keep talking about this until we find some resolution that we both can live with.' Lately I've been able to face the situation and say what

I need when the incident happens rather than storing up my feelings."

Exploring a New Frontier

Still exhilarated by how easy it had been to fly with Jim to a nearby city, Brian used the momentum of his success to take a second flight a little farther from home. After several experiences, with only minor anxiety at takeoff, he was reassured that he could use his skills. He was ready to go on the trip he had canceled seven months earlier. "I pictured the plane as a safe place, reminding myself of the statistics on how safe air travel really is. Going to Europe was wonderful. I continued taking the antidepressant medication and I used all my relaxation skills. For a month we traveled from Amsterdam to Belgium, Florence, Venice, Switzerland, and the south of France. I experienced practically no panic, only brief periods of manageable anxiety."

The most difficult frontier for Brian was communicating his feelings. "I am inexperienced at recognizing my feelings. I have barely cracked that door open. I am just learning to ask myself, 'What do I feel? What in my life is making me anxious or uncomfortable with myself?' For example, I have a wonderful relationship with Jim, but I still have an almost automatic impulse to shut down and withdraw if he does anything that angers or upsets me. He is HIV positive and has periods when he doesn't feel well and is especially irritable. I try to understand what he is going through and not take it personally, but my feelings still get hurt when he is short-tempered with me.

"Recently we moved to a new house. On our second morning there I let the dog out in the back yard. When she came back with muddy paws, Jim started to wipe off her feet. Then suddenly he threw the rag down and stormed into the bedroom without a word. I knew he hadn't been feeling well all week, but the incident escalated in my mind. I became sick to my stomach and resentful that my day had been ruined by his behavior.

"In the past I would have suffered in silence—sometimes for days—feeling rejected and waiting for him to break the ice. This time I realized I was making myself sick, and decided to do something about it. Before leaving for work, I went into the bedroom. All I had time to say was, 'That hurt me,' before he looked up and apologized. 'I'm really sorry. I just washed the dog last night and I was feeling really lousy this morning. I didn't mean to let it out on you.' After that, my tension was gone. What I did *for myself* felt like breaking through a big barrier. If I'm able to trace what is bothering me, and if I'm able to address it, most of the time the anxiety dissipates and my bellyaches go away."

What Does This Have to Do with Me?

When I first heard about the typical characteristics of people suffering from panic and phobias, I was confused. Difficulty asserting oneself? Needing approval? Uncomfortable expressing feelings? But I was outgoing and talkative. I have spoken out in support of political beliefs. I have been able to negotiate in work situations. I often have intense feelings.

Yet, when we shared our experiences in a phobia support group, I saw that we all had a mixture of confidence and insecurity. We were assertive in some situations, but in relationships or situations where we felt emotionally dependent, we were intimidated and awkward about expressing our needs or desires. We were uncomfortable asking for or accepting help without making lengthy apologies. We had a hard time saying "no" unless we accompanied our refusal with guilt-filled explanations and justifications. Although many of us felt our emotions deeply, we were hesitant to express our anger, our grief, or our fear. We were afraid to appear weak or vulnerable. We were sympathetic to the feelings of others, but often didn't know how to distinguish our own responses from their feelings. We often felt *too* sensitive or too easily hurt to face the emotional reactions of others. We observed that these qualities increased our feeling of helplessness. We agreed that our attempts to censor our self-expression contributed to our anxiety.

Most phobia treatment programs include a unit on assertiveness to address these concerns. People who suffer from panic and phobia especially need to learn that asserting oneself is not an act of aggression or a lack of concern for others. Assertiveness means behaving in ways that promote your own dignity and self-respect without violating the rights of others. Since we are acutely sensitive to what other people think (the WPTs), assertiveness skills—which include communication, conflict resolution, and negotiation skills—are especially important to us.

Almost all programs or books on assertiveness include a "bill of rights" that provides a framework for setting boundaries with others and taking responsibility for ourselves. The following statements are typical of the principles represented in most assertiveness programs. Be aware of your own response to each statement. You may find that some of them sound perfectly natural to you, while others surprise you. They may even contradict rules and values you learned as a child.

- I have the right to experience and express my feelings.
- I have the right to say "no," "I don't know," or "I need to think about that."
- I have the right to act without providing excuses or justifications.
- I have the right to change my mind.
- I have the right to put myself first when it feels appropriate.
- I have the right to make mistakes—and be responsible for them.
- I have the right to ignore the advice of others.
- I am not responsible for anticipating the needs of others.
- I have the right to ask for help or emotional support.
- I have the right to ask for information.

These assertiveness guidelines challenged my prohibitions against considering my own needs and desires. Although both men and women struggle with assertiveness issues, women in particular have been conditioned to be polite and pleasing even about basic issues of survival. Although we might prefer everything to be resolved happily, sometimes taking responsiblity for ourselves means going beyond our comfort zone and expressing our voice, whether in a relationship, a legal negotiation, a job promotion, or a sexual harassment complaint.

Learning a New Language

For me, regaining equilibrium on the highway went hand in hand with gaining confidence in my ability to communicate my feelings and ask clearly for what I wanted. My old coping habits of discounting my feelings or holding back my anger paralleled my reluctance to take my rightful place on the road.

I had remarried during the years my phobias were developing. I sincerely appreciated Michael's lack of judgment about my limitations, but I was disturbed by his tendency to sometimes withdraw from me emotionally even though he appeared to be listening. I often felt as though he was trying to mollify me to avoid conflict.

In the past I had felt uncomfortable and awkward approaching someone directly if I had a problem with our interaction. My inclination was to resort to whining or sarcasm if something upset me. By participating in a twelve-step program, I heard other people tell how they handled emotionally charged situations. I learned that I could verbalize my feelings in a way that another person could understand.

One evening while I was trying to tell Michael something, he turned on the television. For a moment I held my breath, clenching my jaw and tensing my shoulders. Then I remembered to breathe, slowly and deeply, intentionally inviting my feelings. When I realized I felt hurt and angry, I turned back to him and said, "Please let me know when you can turn off the set for a few minutes. I want to talk to you when I can have your full attention."

When he came over to me, I told him, "When you turned on the game in the middle of our conversation, I felt shut out and unloved." By coming back to myself, recognizing what I was feeling, and describing those feelings clearly, I was able to engage his attention. As we talked further, he admitted that he *was* trying to shut me out, but not for lack of love or concern. He told me he needed some time after work to cool off and unwind. I appreciated getting that information and then told him that I needed him to be clear about when he could give me his genuine attention and when he couldn't. He understood, and we went for a walk together to continue our conversation. As our communication improved, we both became less threatened by our differences and more relaxed about recognizing and expressing our individual needs.

Several months later, I was overwhelmed by grief after the death of a friend. I would find myself suddenly crying at the dinner table or at random times during the day. Again I felt like Michael was acting unusually cold and distant. One day as he started to leave the room, I called to him to come back. "I feel very alone," I told him. "When you walk away, I feel like you are shutting me out again." He turned back to me and said he felt intimidated by my intense feelings because he didn't know what to do to help me. His honesty helped me understand his experience. "I don't need you to do anything for me," I said. "I can accept what I'm feeling. It would make a difference if you would sit with me for a few minutes, just hold my hand and not say or do anything more. I don't need you to solve a problem; be here with me for a few minutes, just to make contact." "I can do that," he said, relieved. "I was afraid I was supposed to be able to do more."

Breaking an Old Pattern

Kathy did not feel that she had her husband's cooperation in developing communication. Jack was angry at her for not being able to lead a "normal" life; she felt that his impatience made her too uncomfortable to go out with him even when she started getting better. They had reached an impasse in which they maintained a relationship of convenience with little emotional closeness. They communicated only about practical arrangements.

At the same time, Kathy was rebuilding her confidence and self-esteem. With some help from friends, her sister, and her daughter, she was venturing out more and more. She started using her creative talent to develop several craft items, which she sold in local shops. The effect of years of depression began to fade as she became active again, making trips to the store to gather supplies and spending many hours working on her projects. She enjoyed the small profits she was making selling her crafts.

One day Kathy and her husband had a fight. "He was rude and aggressive and thought he had the right to tell me how things were going to be around here!" After he left for work, Kathy acknowledged to herself that unless their relationship changed, she might need to separate from Jack. That afternoon he called from work and asked if they could talk.

That evening, they sat down together to talk. "I told him things I had never said before. I told him he was controlling and manipulative. I got stuff off my chest that I had held in for twenty-two years. I said, 'You get mad and say something that sounds like a question, but you don't really want to hear what I have to say. You start talking and you won't stop and listen to me. I get upset and shut my mouth and don't say anything. I stuff all my feelings and all my anger down inside me. The reason I have remembered so many resentments over the years is because I never told you, "I'm angry," or, "You hurt my feelings." I never had a chance to work things out with you.'

"This time he was really listening. We didn't yell or argue. It was a very good talk, and I felt like we were starting to cover some ground. He took responsibility for things he hadn't even been aware of doing. It's hard for me to have confrontations, but I'm having more respect for myself. Speaking up was a big victory.

"I know you can't change everything overnight, but since then we have been able to talk. We even started to have an argument one night, but we worked it out. Jack has gotten involved in one of my craft projects, and the other day we went together to six stores. On my birthday, we went to a restaurant for the first time in two years. He told me that night that he'd had a wonderful day and really enjoyed being out with me."

Developing Fair Fighting Rules

If talking about your feelings is new to you, you can use as a guide the formula that helped me initiate a discussion with Michael: "When you said (or did) _____, I felt _____." For example, "When you ignored my question, I felt hurt." This simple format can help you focus on a specific event rather than on broad generalizations that feel threatening to the other person but are almost impossible to discuss. By using open-ended questions like, "Can you tell me what was going on for you?" you can learn about the other person and open the way for understanding rather than misunderstanding. You can also build in safeguards by making agreements that provide a structure for handling conflict.

Claire used to be afraid of her husband's anger. As she learned to face her fear, she found new power in expressing herself. "I know now that I am not responsible for Ray's anger, and I don't burst into tears if he's irritated about something. When we have a conflict, we set up definite boundaries for fair fighting. We stick to what is going on right now. We don't bring in other issues from the past. We each get to say what we need to say while the other person listens without interrupting. Our rules and our common desire to be heard make it safe for me to get angry. Though I don't usually yell, I do experience and convey the passion behind my words. We keep reinventing how we want to argue. Sometimes we have post-fight talks to evaluate what helped us and what didn't."

Setting Limits

For some of us, *no* was a bad or dangerous word. Claire admits, "I don't think my lips could form the word *no*! I needed everybody to like me and I didn't want to cause any ripples or waves. But overextending myself and saying 'yes' when I wanted to say 'no' added to my stress and tendency to panic. I began to think of my panic attacks as a signal from me to me, like a buzzer going off to remind me to take care of myself. I made a promise to myself not to wait for that warning signal. Asserting my needs is my way of preventing panic.

"A while ago I got an urgent call from an associate at work, who insisted that she had to see me right away about a problem. In the past I would have rescheduled everything to accommodate her and would even have stayed at work late to get my own job done. She pressured me to see her at lunchtime, but I did not cross over my boundaries. I stayed with my decision without qualifying why I couldn't meet until later in the week. By the time she came to see me, she had handled some of her issues and it was no longer a crisis.

"I've also set limits with my personal acquaintances. I have a dear friend who used to call me in the evening when I was tired. I would stay on the phone, but I had to pinch my arm to keep awake. I thought I was being a good friend, but I wasn't really *with* her because I wasn't honoring myself. By working with my therapist, I developed the ability to express myself. At that time I had no experience saying 'no' out loud, so I would go home and practice with my dog Toby. I would scratch her ears and look her in the eyes and say to her, 'The evening is not a good time for me to be on the phone with you.' My dog took it well, and after practicing with her I was able to say it to my friend. I gave her some better times to reach me, and she is still my closest friend."

My Own Mug of Tea

As Claire became free of her fear of panic, she began to relate to Ray in a different way. She was afraid that if she changed, she would lose her closeness to him. The result was just the opposite. "I know Ray was trying to make life easier for me by trying to read my mind and anticipate what I needed. To me it felt like I had no voice of my own. As I became more confident in myself, I needed to change that.

"Ray and I like to share a mug of tea in the evening. One night we had a big discussion in which I told him that I was ready to assume responsibility for my own voice. 'No one else is responsible for me anymore. I am assuming responsibility for myself, for my panic, for my lack of panic, and I also assume responsibility for saying what I need.' He looked at me for a long time and finally asked, 'Does this mean you want your own mug of tea?' I answered, 'It means that some-times it's okay for us to share and other times I want my own mug of tea.'

"Little by little we discovered the freedom we both have when Ray can be Ray and Claire can be Claire. If Ray is telling a joke, he doesn't have to keep one eye focused on my body language. He can just tell his joke. I have a stronger marriage than I ever thought I could, and we have a deeper, more enduring love for each other. We keep getting closer. But most of all, my relationship with myself has changed. I never knew that I could care for myself so deeply and respect myself so much. That is probably one of the most powerful gifts that panic gave me: changing my relationship with me."

Changing Your Role

When you change your role or behave differently than you did in the past, the fear that originally kept you from speaking up often emerges. It is not uncommon to feel some anxiety at first, along with guilt and even shame for acknowledging your true feelings and needs. If speaking out or negotiating for what is important to you is new behavior for you, you can design a hierarchy similar to the ones you have used to enter physical situations. You can start with little "no's" and small requests before you face more difficult situations. You can send back your food if it is not cooked as you requested, return something to the store, or practice being assertive with a telephone salesperson. You can develop a hierarchy of increasingly challenging opportunities to practice assertiveness and build confidence just as you did in your phobia hierarchies. With each step you will have a chance to discover the actual consequences of expressing yourself. I found out that waiters don't quit if I have a special request, and salespeople are not shocked if I change my mind. Friends go right on breathing if I don't call them immediately, and other people find a way to get where they need to go even if I don't offer to drive them.

As I began to take the risk of setting limits, I got in touch with the feelings and beliefs that had been controlling me. For example, I had always told myself, "I can't let anyone down because I want to be a good person." Looking deeper, I discovered: I want to be needed. My self-esteem is derived from being needed by others. Looking still deeper, I remembered how much I wanted to be loved by my mother. My mother used to tell me that I was the *only one* she could count on to listen to her. I concluded: My mother loves me because I take care of her. That's what gives me value.

To me it became obvious that although my concern for other people is genuine, my inability to set limits for myself stems from the childhood fear that my value and my security depend on making others happy (or, at the very least, making sure they are not unhappy with me). If I let these old beliefs control me, my mature voice gets silenced and I depend on others for my self-worth. When I realize that the root of the fear is in the heart of a little girl who is afraid to lose her mother, it becomes easier to separate my initial emotional reaction from the reality of the present situation. I *can* set limits and voice my feelings to the people in my life. Instead of having to predict, take care of, or control the reactions of others, I can respond in a way that is honest and respectful of myself. When I take responsibility for my needs in my personal life, I feel more confident that I can also take care of myself on the highway.

Touching Your Feelings

Feelings are a form of energy. Unexpressed, this energy becomes distorted and may take the form of anxiety or depression. Yet the energy of our feelings—whether joy, sadness, anger, jealousy, or fear—may not always find an appropriate outlet in the external world. It is not always possible to change a situation that disturbs us. At times we may not wish to confront the person who has triggered strong feelings in us.

In a mindfulness meditation retreat with Buddhist teacher Thich Nhat Hanh, I learned a method of relating to all feelings with compassion, neither withholding nor denying them. Thây (which means "teacher" in Vietnamese) shared with us the metaphor of *touching* our feelings as a loving mother would touch her crying baby. As he writes in his book, *Peace Is Every Step,* "You calm your feeling just by being with it, like a mother tenderly holding her crying baby. Feeling the mother's tenderness, the baby will calm down. . . . The mother is your mindfulness, born from the depth of your consciousness, and it will tend the feeling of pain. . . . The mother has to put aside other things and just hold her baby." He explained that in the same way, we can *touch* our anger, grief, or pain, with love and tenderness.

With this advice, I became less afraid of my feelings. I found that great relief is possible just in the "touching." One day as I was washing the dishes, I thought of an old friend who hadn't responded to my recent letters. I felt anger arise in my body. I didn't resist it or talk myself out of it. I allowed myself to feel it and said to myself, "Oh, this is what anger feels like. I didn't realize I was feeling angry at Carol." At the moment, I wasn't ready to tell her, but in touching my own feelings with acceptance, I regained my peace of mind.

On another occasion, I had had a very busy week and felt wound up and tense. I finally put aside some time to listen to a tape of harp music and do some gentle yoga stretching exercises. After fifteen minutes, my tears started to flow. The tears held no particular content, but they felt like the expression of a voice inside of me that I had overlooked in my rushing around. When I sat up again, my whole body felt relaxed and my anxiety level had decreased. At that moment, I didn't need anyone else to hear me or comfort me. I had taken care of myself. The release of the pent-up emotion left me feeling light and fresh. That afternoon when I drove across the bridge and then took a streetcar to a downtown appointment, my anxiety level was the lowest it had been in weeks—close to zero.

Sometimes it is enough for me to identify my feelings and allow their energy to move through my body.

At other times I need to do something more. I have different ways to take care of myself. If I feel angry, I can beat an old pillow and yell at it; I can exercise intensely to give my body a chance to use the energy that is generated by my feelings; I can write about my feelings in my journal or ask a friend if I can have ten minutes to talk through what is on my mind. I may ask for advice or suggestions, but more often I find that I just need an attentive, noncritical witness so I can hear my own voice. After giving myself time to experience whatever is there, I ask myself, "What do I want or need? Is there an action I need to take? Have I withheld something that I need to communicate?" I don't always know exactly what to say or do, but it becomes clearer when I acknowledge my true feelings.

Respect for your own voice is not measured by how loud you talk or how much you say. It is much more than a mechanical action or statement. It is a commitment to make choices that are are suitable and consistent with your personal integrity and self-esteem. It is an acknowledgment of your value and an appreciation for your own process and timing. With self-respect as your foundation, you *can* take care of yourself in any situation.

How About You?

1. Identify Your Feelings

Instead of judging your feelings, allow them to be the subject of self-exploration. When you feel an emotion, give it a name. Is it anger, sadness, sympathy, excitement? Notice how this feeling affects your body—a knot in your belly, a clenched jaw, an expansion or contraction in your chest? What happens if you don't find some way to express your feeling, either through speaking, using your energy, or taking some action? Write your observations in your journal. Your journal can be part of your support system for articulating feelings.

2. Express Your Feelings

Feelings are normal; feelings are an expression of energy. Experiment with different ways of expressing your feelings that don't depend on another person. For example, if you are angry:

1. Exercise or dance vigorously
2. Beat a pillow or swing a pillow against the couch
3. Breathe deeply into your feeling and "touch" it with compassion
4. Write about your feeling(s) in your journal
5. Write a letter to the person with whom you are upset. Don't necessarily send it, but use it to clarify your feelings.

Communicate Your Feelings in a Non-blaming Way

Ask yourself if you need to communicate with another person. If your feelings are related to something the person did, you can practice using some simple negotiation language. "When you said or did _____, I felt

_____. Can you tell me what you meant? What I would like is _____. How can we work this out?"

3. Write Your Own Bill of Rights

Using the "rights" listed above in this chapter as a starting point, write your own assertiveness bill of rights. Put a check next to the statements that you are ready to implement in your life, and a question mark next to the ones you agree with intellectually but are still not comfortable with. Think about your upbringing as you review each right, and notice if you feel you are entitled to it. Continue to write in your journal as events in your life challenge you to respect your own voice.

4. Create an Assertiveness Hierarchy

Plan an assertiveness hierarchy similar to the desensitization hierarchies you've used for other situations. Set a communication or self-assertiveness goal that you want to accomplish within a specific relationship or situation. Describe at least five steps that could lead to achieving your goal. You can include such steps as talking to a photo, writing an imaginary dialogue with that person in your journal, practicing on your pet, experimenting with a nonthreatening friend, or setting limits with a telephone salesperson.

Part II

The Spirit
of Freedom

Part I has introduced you to the basic cognitive and behavioral skills that are the core of any program to reduce anxiety and panic attacks and to heal from phobias. Each person you have met here has been able to return to a more active life by using the relaxation, thought-changing, and desensitization skills already described.

In the process of altering our fear response, many of us began to see ourselves in a new light. We became aware that our anxiety was often linked to unexpressed grief and loss, or childhood incidents that had undermined our self-esteem. For some of us, this revelation was initially discouraging. We weren't sure if we wanted to examine the deeper issues underlying our behavior. But we discovered that our experience with panic and phobias served us in an unexpected way. By exposing the beliefs and assumptions that had dominated our lives, our crisis actually gave us the opportunity to make new decisions. This has led us to living with choices and expectations that are more relevant to who we are now.

To the surprise of each of us, our wound opened doors to new understandings of freedom.

The stories in Part II, "The Spirit of Freedom," present some experiences that go beyond the scope of a typical cognitive-behavioral program. In order to convey the possibilities for growth and healing, I describe my personal journey in more detail than in previous chapters. I also draw from my experience as a hypnotherapist to address issues that often emerge during the transformation process. If our stories raise questions that relate to your own experience, you may wish to seek the guidance of a counselor, therapist, or support group.

HERE AND NOW

Standing in the here and now
reaching out to you,
I close my eyes
and then I see
It's me I'm reaching to.

—Dale K. S. Ireland

9

Piecing Together the Puzzle

We were relieved to acquire the information and skills that helped us reduce adrenalin, prevent the panic response, and return to situations that had been uncomfortable for us. But sometimes we still asked ourselves, "Why me? Other people are sensitive. Other people think negative thoughts. Other people experience stress. Why did this happen to me?" The exploration of this question often led us back to childhood experiences that shaped our attitudes and beliefs about ourselves, others, and the world around us.

Fear of Loss or Separation

Many of us have experienced an intense fear of separation, which was expressed in our anxiety about being alone or being away from a "safe" person or place. This fear is often rooted in our family histories, in events that made us feel extremely insecure or afraid of being left alone. Some of us suffered a sudden or unexpected death of a parent or other significant family member—a loss made more bewildering if we couldn't talk about our feelings. Others had less obvious traumas but were raised with messages that made the outside world seem like a frightening place or presented an exaggerated view of the risk of physical danger.

I found that as I confronted the day-to-day situations that intimidated me, unexpected memories emerged, revealing pieces of the puzzle of my own history. I discovered that through my phobias, I was acting out unresolved emotional issues from childhood. This awareness helped me come to terms with some of my past feelings, and thus freed me to bring my attention back to what I needed now.

Slipping Back into Avoidance

When I first got Hilda's phone number, I was working in San Francisco as the director of marketing for a graphics firm. Diligently practicing the skills she taught me, I had regained my ability to drive across the bridge to work each morning, even daring to pick up commuters who regularly lined up at bus stops along the way. Sometimes when I left the office in the evening after a hard day, I felt a pang of dread as I settled behind the wheel for the drive home. But my positive self-talk and the classical music on the radio got me through this initial resistance, and, once on the bridge, I was fine.

During this period, my interest and abilities in the human potential movement steadily grew. For many years

I had been teaching evening classes on developing intuition. I found that my sensitivity and empathy (qualities shared by many phobics) enhanced my natural instinct for teaching and counseling. I decided to enroll in a training program that would qualify me to be a clinical hypnotherapist. When I was ready to turn my attention to this new profession, I opened an office in my home and began advertising for clients. I wrote magazine articles, gave talks, and presented workshops, and my practice grew quickly. I loved the work and felt it was a natural way for me to contribute. But the bonus was that I never had to drive to the city. I would listen to the morning commute report and sigh with relief. "Thank God I don't have to go out there. No more traffic, no more bridges for me!"

Once I stopped driving regularly, my phobic avoidance began to take over. By the time six months had passed, I was again afraid to drive to San Francisco. I called Hilda and told her I was in trouble. "Come on over," she said. "You just need to get back on the road." We planned a new hierarchy, including a session of riding together so I could get back my confidence and my realistic thinking. The second time I drove over the bridge with Hilda, I felt almost "normal" again. She was right. Staying away had left too much room for the old fear rehearsals and dread to sneak back in. As I drove onto the highway after crossing the bridge, Hilda congratulated me: "Mani, you've done great. You really are in charge." As I heard those well-intentioned words, my heart started to race. I pulled over to the side of the road and began to cry. "That's it, Hilda! It's terrifying for me to think I'm in charge!"

A Memory

Nothing on the highway was responsible for my strong response. Hilda's words took me back to a memory that had been buried since I was eight years old:

I am sitting next to my mother in our pea-green 1950 Plymouth. A traffic cop has just signaled for her to pull over. As he leans through the window, her rigid composure crumbles. Watching her body convulse with sobs, I wonder, "Who's in charge here?" My father has been dead for six months, and my mother looks like a broken doll. There, at the corner of Hillside Avenue and 144th Street, I make a decision: "I am in charge."

I shook my head to bring my attention back to the present and to the car where I sat, almost in a state of shock, next to Hilda. I told her what I had remembered when she said "in charge." We talked briefly about the incident, then I took a few more minutes to regain my composure by breathing slowly and deeply before turning on the ignition and driving back onto the highway. I was deeply shaken, but this time I knew it wasn't because of the bridge.

The Story in the Photographs

I felt as though a trap door that had been sealed shut against my fear had suddenly sprung open. I realized that the frightened voice that screamed, "Don't make me do this," or, "I can't do it," had always been with me.

It was the same voice I heard when I balked at going out alone or driving any distance. Although it had often filled me with terror and anxiety, I never really heard it as clearly as I did that day.

That evening I dug out some photographs from my childhood. My attention was drawn to an image of my mother sitting on the edge of my bed. I could almost feel the texture of her gray pleated skirt as I remembered:

> *One night when she comes to tuck me in, I try to explain how upset I am because my teacher made fun of me that day in school. "If you only knew how small your problems are compared to mine," Mom tells me. I feel guilty. She has burdens I cannot even imagine. How can I expect her to care about my little problems? She needs my understanding. I have to take care of her so she won't die. I switch to some cheerful small talk and kiss her good night.*

As a result of that incident, I sealed off a fragile and emotionally hungry part of myself. I never really felt like a normal child again. I had always assumed this was because I grew up without a father. Now, as I looked at the photograph of my mother and me, I realized that although my father's death had a dramatic impact on my life, it was my decision to stay in control, to be in charge, that ended my childhood. It wasn't just that my mother didn't listen that night—I also stopped listening to myself.

I was tall and smart, and it was easy for me to act older than my age. Relatives and family friends often commented on my maturity. I saw that my grown-up qualities were valued, and it became harder and harder to admit the fearful thoughts and childish concerns that sometimes plagued me as I tried to fall asleep at night. As I recalled these feelings from the past, I realized that my panic attacks did not come from out of nowhere. They were related to the uneasiness of the child who had remained emotionally trapped while the rest of me grew into an adult. Panic had forced me to hear her cry for help.

My Family History

Both my parents were born in Germany and had left in the thirties to escape the growing persecution of Jews. I met my grandfather on my father's side. He was a tall, stern man who lived with us until his death when I was three. I knew almost nothing about my maternal grandparents, not even their names. Every now and then a glimpse from my mother's childhood slipped out. "My sister and I competed to see who could be thinner. We used to wipe the butter from our bread and stick it on the bottom of our plates. . . . Mother never paid any attention to me. She always left me in the care of housekeepers." Other than those rare comments, my mother's tight-lipped silence made me think that she hated her parents, which was almost impossible for me to imagine because I loved mine so much.

Most of what I know about my family history I learned after both my parents were dead. Soon after I overcame my fear of flying, I went to New York and spent three days interviewing my eighty-one-year-old Uncle Willy. He had known both my parents since childhood and did his best to answer my questions.

My mother, Alice, was the younger daughter of an educated, middle-class family. Her father was a respected dentist who traveled throughout Europe, introducing Western methods of dentistry. But with his immediate family, Max was a domineering, cruel man. He once broke my mother's arm in a fit of rage. He pulled out her hair when she came home late. She feared and detested him. My grandmother, Nellie, was a passive and dependent woman who made no effort to protect her two daughters from their father's abuse. When Max died of a heart attack, she committed suicide by jumping out the second-story window of their home. Left alone and unprepared, Alice, just sixteen, and her older sister, Erika, took what they could and fled from Germany, where they were increasingly threatened by Nazi persecution. They went to several countries and eventually settled in New York, where they dated young men they had known since childhood. Erika married the man I call Uncle Willy, and soon after, my mother married his closest friend, Jacob—my father.

A Sad Story

Until I was seven I had a reasonably comfortable and happy childhood. My favorite memories are of times I spent playing with my older brother. My most distressing memories are of being sent away to summer camp when I was five, and of being treated for a mild case of polio the year I started kindergarten. Then, when I was seven, my father went to the hospital for some tests. The next day my uncle took me aside and told me a sad story. He said that my father had gone away on a long trip. He compared it to a time when he had traveled to Africa and his children did not know when they would see him again. Tears welled up in my eyes because I felt such a sense of loss, but the story was confusing and I didn't know why Uncle Willy was telling it to me. Then it dawned on me. He was telling me that my father was gone. I asked him, "Are you saying that my father is dead?" "Yes," he said. His eyes met mine for a second and the room became very silent. Then he held me while I cried.

When we returned to the rest of the family, we talked about what to have for dinner and what was on television. We talked about everything but my father. I didn't know the cause of his death. I didn't even know he had been sick. Neither my mother nor my big brother said one word about him. I was afraid to ask. I went off to school the next day, business as usual. My grieving for him had lasted only the few minutes I'd cried with Uncle Willy, yet for years I wondered if I had done something that made my father die. Secretly I felt guilty. I also felt sorry for myself, though it didn't ever occur to me to talk to anyone about my pain and confusion.

Our Family Survival Kit

My parents' emotional life was governed by unspoken rules they considered necessary for survival: Forget the past. Don't express your feelings to anyone—lick your wounds in private. Stifle grief and anger. *And no matter what, carry on functioning as usual.* They believed it was pointless to show emotions and that, in fact, it was dangerous to even have strong emotions. Complaining was tolerated, but the expression of real feelings was too frightening to be allowed.

My family's insistence on withholding information and repressing emotions made the world seem like a menacing place. I always felt that there was something I should know, but I could never put my finger on what it was. Forty years later, I asked my uncle what caused my father's death. I found out that his heart had been damaged by childhood rheumatic fever. The adults in the family knew he was a sick man who was often too weak to go to work. "He always seemed to have one foot in this world and one in the next," Uncle Willy told me. "He knew he would probably die young and really didn't intend to have a second child, but when your mother got pregnant, she really wanted you."

My memory is drawn to another photograph. A handsome man in a double-breasted suit is holding a six-month-old child. The child's eyes are focused on him, but he is looking dreamily into space. Some time ago in a therapy group, the facilitator asked me, "Aren't you angry at your father for leaving you?" I was dumbfounded. How could I be angry at someone whose heart failed? But now as I focus on the picture, a lump of undigested anger rises from my stomach. I *am* angry—at a father who didn't tell me that he was sick, who didn't say good-bye. I am angry at a father who didn't have the courage to help me face my pain and left me to grieve my loss on my own.

I know my parents loved me, and I am grateful for all that they gave me, but I still need to acknowledge how their actions and attitudes affected my life. *It's not to find fault with my parents, but only to find myself* that I have struggled to remember and understand what happened to me. Several years after President Kennedy was assassinated, my mother told me, "I'm sorry I didn't let you come to Daddy's funeral. When I saw the Kennedy children on TV, I realized I had made a mistake."

It's a relief to realize that my persistent anxieties did not arise in a vacuum. By recognizing the experiences that shaped my outlook, I have been able to accept what actually happened, and consequently, take responsibility for what I need to heal now.

Meeting the Child

The emotional pain that I could not identify or express did not go away when I ignored it; it found another outlet. It called to me in the seemingly endless flow of tears I cried when an animal died in a movie, or the irrational terror I felt if my daughter was late getting home from school. The unexpressed grief, the denied anger, and the sadness were converted into worry, or expressed as a panicky voice that screamed, "I can't—I won't—I'll die."

I needed to express those feelings without allowing them to take over my life. I needed to understand how suppressed feelings from the past were shaping my responses now. Using a process I learned in my hyp-

notherapy training, I found a format to explore emotions that might otherwise seem threatening or hard to
express. I used guided imagery to meet the child part of
myself who knew how to *act* big but didn't feel very
confident inside.

To begin my process, I prepared myself as I would
for a relaxation session. Sitting in a large stuffed chair, I
covered my lap with a soft afghan. Then I closed my
eyes and took ten minutes to breathe slowly while shift-
ing my attention from my awareness of my surroundings to the feelings and sensations in my body. If I
noticed any tense muscles, I contracted them and then
let go of the tension as I had learned to do in progressive relaxation. Then I allowed my breath to expand the
area around my heart, as though creating a space there
for my scenario to unfold.

In my imagination, I pictured a beautiful garden
with two comfortable chairs, one big and one small, and
I invited my child self to join me there. When I let my
mind float, a five-year-old child appeared, her fingers
wrapped around her long brown braids. She looked
quizzically at me. I asked her if there was anything she
would like to tell me. At first she didn't say anything,
and I accepted her silence. As I continued to relax, she
finally spoke to me in a voice I heard through an intuitive knowing or sensing, rather than hearing with my
ears. I listened. She told me she was scared. She told
me she felt alone. She told me she was tired of trying so
hard, and she was upset that she had become so serious
and didn't really remember how to play. She told me
she didn't want to be in charge.

My body rocked back and forth as I listened to her. Pent-up feelings stirred inside me. Filled with these emotions, I became that child. I consciously let myself experience the feelings. When I felt ready, I purposely shifted my focus and became the adult me again—the listener. By changing roles and being both the child and the adult, I learned that I *did* have some control. I could open to my vulnerable feelings and then I could choose to shift back to my adult center. The feelings of my child self were being cradled in the arms of the adult me.

I repeated this process on several occasions. Sometimes the child appeared as an image from the photographs; other times she seemed to step out of a memory of some event I hadn't thought about for decades and was surprised to remember. I didn't try to *do* anything. I didn't try to change anything. I just said to her, "I love you and I want to know you better. Is there anything else you want to tell me?"

As I uncovered my feelings in this way, I came to understand how they related to a time in my childhood when I really was dependent on the care of others, a period when separation from my mother or father felt life-threatening. Until I identified the actual source of my fearful and insecure feelings, I mistakenly assumed that their intensity was directly related to whatever was happening to me in the present. Now I realized that the source of my fear was actually my terrified childhood feelings. This made my fear less threatening to me. I didn't have to steel myself and clench my teeth to hold back my feelings. I could turn to my child self and say,

"I know you are afraid. I care about you and will stick by you. Let me hold your hand."

Don't Give Her the Keys to the Car

The next time I needed to drive to San Francisco, I heard the voice in my head saying: "I don't want to do this. Don't make me do this." Whereas in the past this voice would have been enough to make me turn around and go home, this time I heard my cry for help in a new way. Instead of identifying with the voice, I imagined it belonged to a child sitting next to me in the car. I pictured her as a very relaxed Raggedy Ann doll leaning against my hip. I said to her, "I know that you're too little to drive this car. Your feet don't even reach the pedals and you can't see over the dashboard. I want you to know that you don't have to take charge. I promise I won't make you do anything you don't want to do. I'm grown-up and well coordinated. I have been driving for twenty years. I can handle it. You don't have to do it, little child. You can rest in my heart and I will drive the car."

This dialogue pulled me back to the reality of driving. I focused my attention on the road. I felt the breeze on my arm. I saw the maroon color of my seats and felt the smooth surface of the steering wheel in my hand. This gave me some detachment from the fear thoughts. I used my skills for stopping thoughts and relaxing the body, but I no longer felt like I was fighting an enemy. I understood that many of my fear thoughts were remnants from the past. This made me feel safer stopping those thoughts. I wasn't rejecting myself. I wasn't rejecting my hurt inner child. I was rejecting these habitual thoughts that served no purpose but to overstimulate my nervous system. I could love the scared child within me, but I didn't have to give her the keys to the car. My adult self was in charge.

Filling Out the Memories

Another way of making contact with your inner child is by investigating your family history. Although this information will not, by itself, cure your phobias, it can help you uncover the source of your beliefs and fears. It may also help you reconnect with some of your original childlike enthusiasm for life. You can stimulate your memory by looking at photographs and gathering information from those who knew you when you were growing up. If you have living relatives or family friends, you can learn a lot about your history, both from what they say and how they say it. Their recollections may not accurately reflect your experience, but can still help you get a perspective on family attitudes and viewpoints that influenced you.

Encouraged by my own emerging memories, I wrote a letter to my brother, Tom, asking him if he could tell me how he remembered me as a child. Although he and I had never corresponded before, this time I got back a three-page letter. The first paragraph read: "When I think of you as a young child, I remember a lively little girl, alert, laughing, easy to please and make happy. I felt that with Daddy's death you began a long detour. But I see you today as becoming once again an adult version of that beautiful child."

Acceptance

I framed a sweet photo of myself taken at age four, before my hair was cut short for kindergarten. Looking at it helped me be more patient with myself. I didn't want to push this little girl, judge her, or ridicule her— which meant I couldn't do those things to myself.

This attitude made it easier for me to approach my hierarchies, even if I sometimes felt like a beginner again. I continued my daily relaxation practice and took whatever steps I could as I faced the ordinary situations in my life. Pretending there was still a little child inside who was affected by my attitudes helped me live with my temporary limitations. Whether or not I was able to move into a faster lane and pass a truck, whether or not I drove all the way to the tunnel, I congratulated myself as I would have congratulated her. I gave myself credit for what worked, for everything I did, rather than focusing on what didn't happen the way I had hoped. I stopped saying to myself, "I drove to Walnut Creek *but* . . ." Whether I pulled over or brought a friend along, the victory counted. "I drove to Walnut Creek" was enough.

I was healing an old wound by being patient with myself. Understanding what I experienced growing up made me want to treat myself with more kindness now. Practicing my skills became less of a burden and more enjoyable. I became comfortable rewarding myself with praise, with gold stars on my victory chart, with flowers.

Losing Her Mother:
Claire's Family Secret

When Claire started working with a therapist to change her panic response, she learned that one of the background characteristics common to people with phobias is secrecy about significant family experiences. "It hit me—the only thing I'm keeping secret is my mother!"

Claire was the oldest of three children in a very close-knit family. She remembers her early childhood as a happy time and recalls being excited that her parents were planning to adopt a fourth child. She adored her mother, who always made her feel very special and loved. Then, when Claire was in sixth grade, her mother, grandmother, and younger brother were hit by a car while crossing the street. "At the time, I was sitting in a Kaiser hospital waiting room with my dad and sister because I had injured my neck doing tumbling at school. Someone called my father out and a little later he came back into the room. 'Your mother, grandmother, and brother have just been in a car accident,' he told us. 'That's why you always have to look both ways when you cross the street.'

"I don't remember all the details after that, only that we sat in hospital waiting rooms and ended up at an aunt's house, where the phone kept ringing. We didn't quite understand what was going on. My sister and I were watching TV and eating Kentucky Fried Chicken when my dad came in. My sister remembers him telling us that Mom had died. I can't remember the words, only the feeling inside. I remember the smell of chicken and the feeling of everything stopping."

Claire thought it would be unbearable for her father to live without his wife. She asked him if he was going to commit suicide to be with her mom. "I remember him trying to respond to me by saying he would never do that, but he wasn't really there. He was so grief-stricken; he was holding his head in his hands. I think I felt that it was my fault, that somehow I made this happen. Maybe if I hadn't needed to go to the doctor that day . . .

"We were staying with relatives and I just wanted to get back home so I could take care of things. I thought, 'If we can just get home, I'll make sure we go to school. I can cook. I can make hot-dog stew. I'm going to take charge. I'm going to fix things and everything is going to be okay.' I needed to get back some sense of control because I had no feeling of control at all—not over my body, not over my tummy being upset. I was afraid to be alone with my thoughts. I remember my father would come and sit down on my bed at night and say, 'Your feet are relaxing, your legs are relaxing . . .' but I couldn't sleep."

Over the next several months, Claire and her sister and father spent hours at the hospital with her brother, who was in a coma. While sitting by his bedside, they talked about her mother and shared their memories of her. Eight months later, just before her brother came home from the hospital, her father remarried. "We moved into a new house where there were no pictures of my mom anywhere. It became a big secret that I had

had a mother whom I loved very much and that she was gone now. I felt it wasn't safe to mention her name because that would upset my stepmother. I needed desperately to be loved, so I had to be the good daughter. I was willing to change myself so my stepmother would love me, and that meant deserting my mom—and, I see in hindsight, deserting myself.

"I'm convinced that this contibuted to making my experience of panic so intense. To understand my panic, I had to look beyond my fear of riding in elevators and search deep inside of myself. What I found was this little kid who had lost her mother and felt alone and abandoned."

Claire decided to visit places she had been with her mother. Her mother had worked as a librarian at the local library. "I went there and opened up books with her handwriting in them. I walked around rejoicing in the memories I had of being with her. Sometimes I took a photograph of my mother with me, because it gave me an incredible feeling. Holding her picture, I felt as though we were walking up the stairwell together."

Her Face in the Mirror

While waiting for an appointment with her doctor, Claire had an experience that helped her transform her fear of being alone and not able to take care of herself. "I was sitting in the waiting room on the tenth floor of a medical building. I didn't feel secure and began thinking, 'What if I need to get out of here?' I wanted someone to take care of me. I wanted someone to make those feelings go away. As my panic started escalating, I looked up and I saw my reflection looking back at me from the mirror. At that moment, I had the profound realization *that I wasn't alone.*

"Ever since that day, I have had a sense of power and confidence. The child inside me was looking in the mirror for someone to be there and she found a trustworthy adult who answered, 'I am here. You are not alone.' My panic attacks have been the reaction of someone who needed to be taken care of. In that moment at the mirror I instantly knew that that's what I can do for me. I take care of myself. I use my breathing when I need to, but most often I don't need to count or do anything special to prevent panic. If I ever start to feel uncomfortable, I look down at my hands and know that I'm here and that I am able to take care of myself. When I started driving over bridges, I'd flip down the mirror on the visor or look in the rearview mirror and say 'I am not alone, I'm still here.' Instead of making Ray my safe person, I found my safe person in the glass that day, looking back at me."

Healing the Separation

Many of us have restricted our range of activity or relied on someone else to hold our hand. This isn't because we really fear the outside world or the lack of oxygen in a room. What underlies our fear of being alone, being exposed, or losing control has more to do with loss—loss of another or loss of some part of ourselves. By embracing our feelings and the truth of our experience, we have found ourselves once again.

Whether or not you have lost a parent or loved one, an exploration of your family history can provide you with significant clues to the question, "Why me?" Though you cannot change the past, you can alter the effects it has on you today. You can acknowledge and integrate parts of yourself that need to be heard. As you grow to trust the competent and caring adult in you, you can take the car keys from the frightened little child inside and proceed on your journey.

How About You?

1. Dialogue with Your Inner Child

Use the "Guide for Listening to Your Inner Child" beginning on page 286. In the beginning, you may want to record it on a tape player, leaving yourself at least a couple of minutes after each instruction. Then sit in a comfortable chair and close your eyes. Use your breathing or progressive relaxation to become calm. When you are ready, turn on the tape and follow the directions.

If you want the emotional support and guidance of an experienced person, contact a professional counselor or therapist who does inner child work or guided visualization.

2. Family History

Gather photographs from your childhood and pick out the ones that catch your attention. Use your memory and imagination to describe what is happening in the photo. How does the child in the photo feel? What might she or he want to tell you? Don't restrict yourself to what you "know" as fact; let your imagination read into the image and find out what it may reveal about your feelings.

Write a letter to someone who knew you as a child—a relative, sibling, or family friend. Ask how that person remembers you as a child. You might learn something from getting several viewpoints.

3. Supportive Self-Talk

Think about what words you always longed to hear when you were growing up. Did you want your father to tell you that he really loved you? Do you wish your mother had complimented you on your artistic talent? Did you wish they were more interested in your feelings, hopes, and dreams? Write down in your journal all the positive affirmations that your loving, caring adult self would say to your child inside. Look in the mirror and say them out loud to yourself every morning and evening for a week. You can also record these acknowledgments and play the tape for yourself before you go to sleep.

10

Changing Core Beliefs

The core beliefs that develop during our childhood become the foundation for how we interpret our experiences for the rest of our lives. Some of our beliefs are supportive and valuable to us, contributing to our sense of value and self-confidence: "I am lovable." "My feelings are important." "I'm a fast learner." We also have self-defeating beliefs and rules of conduct that undermine our self-esteem and inhibit our natural abilities. "Nothing I do is ever good enough." As we experience freedom from our phobias and return to the everyday situations of life, we realize that we want more than the ability to function. We want to express our full potential and live with joy. To make this a reality, we may need to identify, evaluate, and change some of our core beliefs.

Feeling Like an Impostor

Edward believes that a sequence of events in his early school years led to the feelings of shame and uneasiness that made his phobias so difficult to confront. "In A.A. meetings I heard people tell stories about what their parents had said or done to them that made them feel worthless or ashamed. I looked through my family's photo album and tried to remember events that had shaped my childhood. Though we had some problems, I couldn't find the source of my shame in my immediate family. I felt loved and had a close relationship with both parents. I was finally able to trace my shame to something that had happened to me in the third grade. That's when I first started feeling like a fraud. From then on, I lived with the gnawing fear that I would be caught and exposed."

Edward is matter-of-fact as he describes the dominant socioeconomic conditions in his school during the 1950s. "The school system got $58 reimbursement per day for retarded children and only $28 for other students. To get more money, my school classified me, along with a handful of other Latino and minority students, as mentally retarded."

In first grade Edward was placed in a classroom in which the special education children, including some who were retarded or emotionally disturbed, were seated in two rows on the right side of the room. They were separated from the regular students by a strip of linoleum. Edward adjusted pretty easily. "I accepted the label and made the best of it. We didn't get any academic training, but I could look forward to recess and I got along pretty well with the other kids." Edward was very interested in books, so he taught himself to read at home. He remained in this handicapped group until one day in the middle of third grade when his teacher went on maternity leave.

"On the day my teacher left, I missed the morning session because I had a dentist appointment. When I got back to school, I discovered that the new teacher had dismantled the rows and rearranged the room into clusters of eight desks. There was no longer a clear separation between the retarded kids and the regular students. The new teacher noticed me and asked, 'Who are you?' 'I'm Edward,' I said, and we talked for a few minutes. Then she pointed to a desk and said, 'Sit over there and do your reading.' I wanted to say to her, 'Wait a minute, I don't do reading. I belong over in the right-hand rows.' I was going to explain to her that I was in the group that doesn't read, but the words didn't come out.

"Once in the reading group, I fit in well, and the teacher kept me there. I thought to myself, 'This is neat. I'm having fun. I enjoy this reading stuff.' But at the same time a new thought started bothering me all the time. 'It won't last. Someone will come along and grab me by the scruff of my neck and say, "Okay, that was fun, but now you're going back where you belong."'

"Although we were told that Mrs. Taylor wasn't coming back, I kept expecting her to show up and be shocked to find me in a new group. The following year I went on to a fourth-grade class and the teacher again separated the 'special' rows, but he put me with the regular kids. I went all through fourth grade with this fear hanging over my head: 'They are going to catch up with you and pull you over there to the retarded rows.'

When it didn't happen in the fourth grade, I waited for the ax to fall in the fifth grade.

"When I started having panic attacks in my senior year of high school, my feeling of humiliation hooked right in to the old fear of being found out. I felt like the fog had lifted and the real truth about what was wrong with me was obvious. It had never been about mental ability at all. The issue was my inadequacy—my inherent flaw was a lack of courage. 'You're a coward,' I told myself. 'And if you can see it, other people can see too. They just have to look at your face and see it written across your forehead.' The other guys in high school saw me freak out on the catwalk on our school trip. I thought it was only a matter of time before everyone would find out that I couldn't drive without sweating and clutching the wheel. The fundamental shame that developed in third-grade now had a face I could not hide. My self-esteem plummeted."

While searching for answers in his phobia group, Edward connected his fear of being stuck in traffic, where people would be able to see him, to his core belief that anyone who looked at him could see that he was inadequate. "The idea that I was inadequate felt true because it had become such an integral part of my experience. Intellectually analyzing the situation was not enough to change the belief. What did make a difference was changing my behavior. Both TERRAP and A.A. call it 'practicing positive behaviors' or 'acting as if' I really valued myself. At first it seemed artificial, but slowly my positive attitude and self-affirming behavior gave me a new sense of myself that was stronger than the old belief. If the inadequacy thoughts came up, I acknowledged them as from the past, but I stopped feeding them with shame. The old beliefs and self-judgments don't stick anymore. Over time, they have almost dropped out of my thinking patterns.

"In fact, now that I have sorted out the root of my shame, I can accept a broader range of feelings and thoughts without using them against myself. For example, I can experience regret, without turning it into self-blame or guilt. I made a decision in graduate school that I regret. In the past, this thought could have turned into a reason to get depressed and put myself down. Now I have a thought, look at it, and then go on to something else."

While talking to me, Edward became choked up. Speaking about his childhood pain had brought up grief: "It's a memory in my mind, but my body has a memory too. Although I know that I am thinking of something that is over, my body still feels the pain. I've learned that once I accept the feeling, in this case the grief, then the emotion lives out its cycle and will pass naturally. When I first started working on my panic, I felt like I had to be careful and exclude all negative thoughts or painful feelings. Today I am not living on the edge anymore, so I can go out to the edges and include all feelings in my experience."

Learning Shame

While Claire was working with a therapist about the feelings connected to her phobias, she became increasingly aware of the shame she felt about not being able to walk up a stairway or do other everyday things. As she got better, she realized that the feelings of shame were not restricted to phobic situations. She identified a core belief that related to her body image and femaleness—a belief that it wasn't okay to be a sensual, sexual woman.

"I remembered a stage in my life when I was about twelve and my body was starting to change. When I first developed breasts and hips, I would look at myself in the mirror and feel happy. I got my period one day at school. I wasn't completely unprepared because my mother had explained it to me before she died. She said that it was special and was part of becoming a woman. But I was still scared and felt confused, so I decided to skip the afternoon class.

"When I got home from school, my stepmother yelled at me. She told me this wasn't a big deal and I shouldn't be so emotional. I felt ashamed of my feelings and never again was comfortable asking her questions or talking about my femaleness or sensuality. My step-mother often insinuated things about my body and made it sound like I had done something wrong. She told me I couldn't sleep in a T-shirt in case my father came in to say good night, and she made it sound like I was trying to seduce him. I didn't always understand what she was implying but I knew that she considered my femaleness a threat.

"I only lived with my stepmother for four years before I moved out, but making her love me was still very important to me. I think I started gaining weight because it made me feel safer. When I look back now, I realize that I wasn't really fat then, though that was my self-perception. When I left home at sixteen, I went to work in a fast-food place and really started to put on weight."

When Claire first recognized her feelings of shame about her body, her thoughts naturally went to her relationship with her stepmother. However, as she continued to talk about her childhood, she remembered an earlier incident that had deeply affected her. It occurred while her birth mother was still alive. When Claire was seven, she was riding on a bus during a day-camp outing. "There was an older boy who worked at camp who used to play with us. Sometimes he would trace the outline of a letter on my back and I was supposed to guess what he had written. One day he sat next to me on the bus and he put his hand in my underpants and then his finger in my vagina. I remember sitting there and being scared, upset, angry, and also really confused.

"Later I told my mother how I felt. I thought that when he finished doing this other thing, he would go back to writing letters on my back. I had good feelings mixed with bad ones. I can picture my mother and me in our living room, and I remember her eyes filling up with tears as she listened to me. The next thing I remember is telling a police officer what had happened. I was sitting next to my mom on a love seat in our home, with the sun warming my back. My mother had her hand on my arm. As I spoke I became more and more aware of the expression on the officer's face. Then, something inside my body froze. I had the feeling that what I had done was wrong and that the whole incident was my fault. Even my mother's caring hand on my arm was not enough to stop the awful feeling inside me.

"I know that the original shame from my childhood experiences fed the phobia. I can't completely explain the connection, but a feeling of abandonment is tied in with shame. I don't remember having actual panic attacks, but after that incident I couldn't get on a bus to go to school. If I couldn't get a ride in the car, I cut school."

Claiming Her Body

Claire was able to change her core beliefs about her body, and she developed a loving and accepting attitude toward herself as a woman. She believes this change unfolded naturally as she discovered that everything is interrelated. "For many years I only wore shirts or sweaters that came down to my knees and covered my body. At first, I wouldn't undress in front of my husband. But every part of my life is an outgrowth of my attitude toward myself. In my phobia work, I stopped thinking of myself as broken and just started to change one aspect of my life at a time, like letting myself touch an elevator door. As I began to let go of the phobia-related shame that had lived in my secret place, my shame about other aspects of myself began to dissolve. When I changed the way I interacted with myself, I opened up. I switched from bossing myself around and talking negatively to myself to nurturing myself. I started releasing many of the feelings and ideas I had held on to and had thought, 'This is who I am.' I was letting go of the image I had built according to everybody else's standards. It was almost as though my hands opened and I could reach for other things. ᵟ

"Looking at memories has been very powerful for me. By using my memories, I'm giving myself self-knowledge and a new perspective. I can make connections that I couldn't make otherwise—understanding what a seven-year-old perceived in contrast to what I see now as an adult. This beautiful new lens brings understanding to my memories and helps me understand why the phobias could take such a hold. I have had to do a lot of unlearning to discover what's true for me now.

"Some of the physical weight is still with me, but I feel like a snake who is getting ready to shed her skin and show how shiny and bright she is. My whole way of thinking has changed. I'm wearing clothes that I never dreamed of wearing. For the first time, I'm going out with friends to clubs where you have to dress up. Recently a coworker noticed that I was wearing more fitted clothes and letting my figure show. She told me I looked fantastic, and I felt it. I'm rock climbing and hiking and riding my bike and doing physical things that I did not do before. I hiked in shorts and loved the feeling of the breeze on my legs and the pounding of my heart. A year ago my heart rate would have terrified me because it would have been related to panic. Now I believe that it is okay to be me, and that includes being a woman. I walk by the mirror and smile at myself. I've stopped looking to the future and hoping that someday

I will be different and that then I'll like myself. I live in the present and enjoy myself right now."

*

Transforming a Core Belief

Some of our conditioned beliefs can be changed by using objective, logical observation. We know that we have done a good job, been a trustworthy friend, or handled a crisis in a responsible way. Even if a parent once said we'd never amount to anything, or a sister seemed to get all the compliments in our family, we recognize our ability and innate goodness and feel released from those negative messages by our own experiences.

Other beliefs are harder to transform because they form the foundation of our self-image and beliefs about ourselves. We have accepted them as unquestionable truths. We are afraid to change them or give them up. I find it helpful to imagine the part of us who is afraid as the frightened child. This child lives in the subconscious mind and believes that the decisions she made are still necessary for her survival. In order to change core beliefs, it is sometimes necessary to free ourselves from the emotional hold of significant early experiences.

Certain forms of therapy are especially effective in helping an individual discover and change core beliefs. A hypnotherapist can lead you through a guided visualization called a regression, which takes you back to incidents from the past that caused you to lose trust in your abilities or your worth. Once you've looked at the memories with a new perspective, you can incorporate positive, healing suggestions and new rules that build self-esteem and self-confidence.

I worked with my own core beliefs using the Transformation Process. This technique was taught to me by my friend and teacher Jeru Kabbal. Though simple to do, the Transformation Process reflects a profound understanding of how the conscious and unconscious mind can work together to transform negative messages and core beliefs. The technique is similar to changing a fear rehearsal to a success rehearsal. Using visualization, it creates a personal experience that was previously lacking, and anchors it to kinesthetic cues to embody a new understanding of ourselves. Although it is sometimes done with the guidance of a therapist, you can also follow this model on your own.

The Transformation Process has two stages. In the first stage, you recall a childhood event in which you learned a self-defeating belief. You narrate the story out loud, using the present tense and speaking in the first person. In the second stage, you invent a *new* story about the event, altering the details to create an alternative experience that conveys a supportive, confidence-building message.

I wanted to transform my core beliefs that my feelings were stupid and that I was too helpless to do new things on my own without feeling terrified. I hoped to replace them with the positive belief that by expressing my feelings, I can take care of myself, and consequently feel confident when embarking on new experiences.

I spent a few days thinking about times in my childhood when I felt particularly anxious or unhappy, and I jotted down several occasions that came to mind. Then I chose the incident that was most vivid in my memory and used it as the subject for the Transformation Process.

Changing the Impact of a Past Event

Stage One: I raise my right forearm. I tell the story briefly, as I remember it. I speak in the present tense and feel my emotions as I relive it.

> *I am nine years old and my mother tells me that her friend Honey has invited me to the circus. Without asking me, my mother has already arranged to put me on the train at our subway stop so Honey can pick me up four stops later. I am filled with dread. I say in a whisper, 'I don't wanna do it.'*
>
> *My mother pooh-poohs my reluctance, telling me: 'Other kids your age ride the train.' I feel ashamed of my fear and too embarrassed to put my real concerns into words. I can't admit that I feel helpless, that I'm afraid I won't be able to find Honey, scared that I might be harassed by a stranger. I don't know why I have these fears, but I get the idea that I am being silly and wrong. My mother puts me on the train. I feel tense all day and I hate the circus.*

After visualizing this scene, I lower my arm and take a few deep breaths. I ask myself what beliefs or decisions I made based on this experience. I come up

with the following beliefs, which, I notice, are also connected to my phobic behavior.

I can't tell anyone what I'm feeling or I will be
humiliated.

I can't ask for help.

I have to push myself whether I'm ready or not.

I must hold my breath so I won't lose control and
embarrass myself.

Stage two: I raise my left forearm. I retell the
story, again speaking in the present tense so I can live it
as I speak. This time I revise the story and create a positive emotional experience which generates different
messages.

*I am nine years old. A friend of the family calls to
invite me to the circus. My mother asks me if I
would like to take the subway to Forest Hills to go
out with Honey. When I express hesitation, she
encourages me to tell her more. I say that I would
like to see the circus, but have never ridden alone
on the subway and am afraid of getting lost or that
someone will molest me. Mom is sympathetic to my
concerns, and suggests that I will probably feel
safer once I see the actual situation. She tells me
that on Saturday afternoon the train is usually full
of families.*

*When I express some interest in going, she
asks me if I would like any help from her. I tell her
I would like her to get on the train with me so I
can decide for myself if I feel comfortable. She
agrees to go with me and offers a plan. We make a*

game out of it. Up to the first stop, I sit next to her. As I look around, I see that everyone seems pretty ordinary and I breathe more easily. We agree that after the first stop, Mom can move to the next car and give me a chance to practice sitting by myself. If I am ready to go on alone, I'll wave to her and she'll get off the train and let me continue on my own for the remaining two stops.

At this point, in creating my new scenario, I breathe deeply. I allow myself to really experience the feeling of being nine years old, sitting on the train, and peeking at my mother in the next car. I don't decide the outcome ahead of time. When I make my decision to go on alone, I continue the story.

I arrive at the second station and wave good-bye to my mother with a big smile on my face. I am excited about my independence and can't wait to tell Honey about the families I observed on the subway. The circus is fun, but the train trip is almost the best part of the day. I like knowing that I can go places on my own if I want to.

When I finish my new story, I rest my arm. I feel happy and my body is relaxed. I have built a positive emotional association with becoming independent. My experience has given me new beliefs to live by.

My feelings are important.

I can ask for help.

I can work toward self-sufficiency at my own pace.

I enjoy my independence.

I end the Transformation Process by raising both arms simultaneously for a few seconds, then letting them come to rest on my heart. With this exercise, I have constructed an inner model that allows me to feel that I can take care of myself in a new situation. I have changed a painful memory into a supportive one. As I raise both my forearms simultaneously, I notice that the original memory does not seem to weigh so heavily on my heart.

We do not use this process to deny what really happened to us, nor can we change the past. But we can change the *impact* of past destructive experiences so their shadow does not distort our reactions to current situations. I knew the second story was made up, but I felt real feelings of relief and self-confidence as I told it. Over time I notice that my experience in this process seems to change my automatic responses. The old memory and the painful feelings that went with it do not control me as they once did.

Dropping Perfectionism and Trusting Yourself

As Kathy began to trust herself again, she found that the rules by which she had lived her life no longer supported her. "After Dad died, my mother had three children to support and raise by herself, and she became very strict with us. She told us we'd better learn to do things right if we wanted to be accepted. I carried that pressure into my adult life—to get it right and make everything look perfect. When I got married, I always wanted my house to be immaculate. I would look for things that were wrong. I think the pressure I put on myself and the fear of falling short added to my anxiety.

"Now I know there is more to life than cleaning the house and getting everything right. The need for perfection was constantly demeaning and damaged my self-esteem. After so many years of trying to be perfect, it's hard to change this pattern, but I'm doing it. Facing my phobias made me realize that finding out who I am is really important to me."

Kathy has begun to challenge her belief that she would not survive if she confronted those she loved. "In childhood and in my marriage, I was always stifling myself because I was so afraid of conflict. I believed, 'If I confront you, you might not love me anymore, so I'll shut my mouth and I'll keep my feelings hidden inside. That's better than to risk losing you.' Now I have started to depend on myself and stand up for myself. I'm not willing to let my husband tell me what to do anymore, and he doesn't always like the way I've changed. But I need to know I can trust myself. *I count. My feelings count.* It all comes down to that.

"When I decided to make a craft line for Christmas—decorative painted clay figures—Jack didn't want me to do it. He didn't think I could make it work. But I made my own decision. I thought I *could* do it. I used two hundred dollars from money I had made selling other craft items. I figured I had the right to take the risk.

"When Jack saw how many orders I was getting, he actually got behind my project and helped. We made many trips to different stores to get supplies, and we set up a system in the garage. He was worried because the designs didn't come out identical each time, but I had fun doing something different now and then. I told myself, 'If I make a mistake, so what. It gives them a little different character.' I don't want to do that old criticizing of myself anymore. It's a losing battle and it takes all the enjoyment out of everything." Kathy sold sixteen hundred dollars' worth of merchandise and felt a real sense of accomplishment. "I feel like now this new person is coming out, and I want her to come out. I want to know who she is. My job of raising my daughter is done and now I want to make room for me."

Changing the Rules

Next to the diplomas and awards in Howard Liebgold's office sits a framed photo of him as a four-year-old child. When I asked why he had the picture there, he told me: "That little vulnerable child was at the mercy of what he was told growing up. From the time he was four, he heard, 'If you don't become a doctor, your grandfather will turn over in his grave.' The other message I got from my mother was that the world was a dangerous place and I might not be able to take care of myself: 'Watch out—be careful out there—don't go too far from home—don't get hurt.' If you're born sensitive and imaginative, that programming is devastating."

When Howard describes his childhood, he first acknowledges that he had two parents who cared about him. "I came from a pretty functional home. My dad was a kind person; he wasn't abusive, abrasive, or alcoholic. He didn't cheat on anybody. But all he did was work. He was a salesman and was gone six or seven days a week. My mother was a very intelligent woman, ahead of her time in that she worked outside the home as a bookkeeper. However, she was also phobic, never learned how to drive, and was overprotective. She taught me to perceive the world in a fearful way.

"I couldn't even have dreamed of being a macho motorcyclist. She refused to sign me up for football because she didn't want me to get hurt. She was very concerned when I played baseball. I remember one time when I was playing shortshop and I got hit in the face with a baseball. I came home with a swollen cheek and a bloody nose, no worse for wear, but mother said something like, 'Someday I'm going to find you dead on the doorstep!'"

Although Howard considers himself cured of his phobias, giving new options to his child self is still an important part of his life. "That little rascal had no idea that he would grow up to be powerful and strong and have choices. I need to remind him of these qualities that I have as an adult. For example, a couple of months ago I was invited to do a television interview. My biggest worry was not about giving the talk; it was about finding my way to a place I hadn't been before. So I told this little guy inside, 'We will leave in plenty of time. I can make a phone call. I can stop and ask for directions.' Once when I got lost in a foreign country, I told him, 'Don't worry, we have a Visa card, we have money and the address of the hotel. All we have to do is give the cab driver this piece of paper and we won't be lost anymore. Anyway, being lost is an adventure and adventures are fun.'"

But Howard didn't challenge the rules he grew up with until two major events forced him to examine the programs that were stored in his brain. "The first time I got into my 'brain in a bag' was when I took the phobia class and began to see how I was controlled by the What Ifs and WPTs. I went even further when I was diagnosed with cancer."

In October 1984, Howard graduated from the phobia class and considered himself cured. Five months later, he was diagnosed with malignant melanoma and underwent immediate radical surgery. "I had finally gotten my life back and all of a sudden I had cancer. I thought that was unfair. It was devastating. Yet in the long run it had the most profound and wonderful result—it gave me back my passion for life. I was suddenly willing to reevaluate everything I did by asking the question, 'What would you do if you knew you were going to die soon?' Using that inquiry, I changed the rules in almost every area of my life.

"I grew up during the Depression, so I learned that I got love and attention for working and bringing money into the household. At fifty-four I was still living by that program. I was the first one in my family to go to college. I became a doctor. I was working all the time and never spent any money. Instead of real vacations I used to take long weekends—Friday afternoon off once in a while. At the end of the year I'd get paid for my accrued vacation time. I worked even more after my divorce in 1981. I was a hermit who became the most productive physician in the history of mankind. I would tell people, 'My vocation is my favorite hobby.' I wrote manuals and articles and stayed at work until seven or eight o'clock every night. That was a great way of staying away from people and from phobic situations—my divine avoidance.

"After getting cancer, I changed all that. What I learned from facing my own mortality was that the other obligation you have for being on this Earth is to have some fun. In the ten years since I was operated on, I've gone on thirteen cruises, plus at least one extra mini vacation every single month. Each year I end up owing Kaiser a couple of vacation days. My goal in life is to die owing Kaiser vacation time. They'll have to dig me up to get it back!

"I also changed my rule about spending money on myself. In the past, I could give money to causes or to other people, but I couldn't give it to me. I had been living in a one-bedroom condo. I was driving a Chevy Chevette. As soon as I was well again, I put a large down payment on a five-bedroom home. After my car was stolen while I was attending the L.A. Olympics, I bought a new Chrysler and a colorful wardrobe. It was a rebirth. As a phobic, I used to dress like a Smurf. I never wanted to bring any attention to myself by dressing well. I wore a blue shirt, blue pants, blue tie, and a $9.95 Timex sport watch. I left my nice watches in the drawer. It was another way of not regaling myself. I began to wear my jewelry and flashy ties. If tomatoes were $1.20 a pound, I used to do without them. I now say, 'Buy the damn tomatoes.'

"I changed my rules about my social life. After getting divorced, I didn't go out very much because I didn't want to get involved. Commitment would mean I would lose my freedom to avoid life. But one of my hierarchies to cure my phobia included increasing my social life. I went to Arthur Murray Dance Studios, which offered classes and mixers where you could meet people. I signed up for a ballroom dancing class, and went up to the teacher before the first lesson and explained to her that I was claustrophobic about feeling trapped with a partner. She smiled at me and said, 'I understand. I'm phobic about doctors.' I felt more at ease after that.

"I discovered that I was a good dancer and kept trying other classes. I went on from social dancing to a tap dancing class. I was very attracted to the teacher, Carol. In the past I would never have asked out my dance teacher because I thought if we broke up she would look unfavorably at my steps, watch for my mistakes, and I would have to quit the class. But after having faced cancer, I said to myself, 'What the hell's the difference? If I'm going to die, I can date anybody I want!' That really freed me. I not only dated Carol, we got married and went on to win four trophies on a dance band cruise.

"The real change in me was that I realized I had never really loved myself before, and now I gave myself permission to love and appreciate myself. I didn't need anybody else's confirmation of my uniqueness or my greatness. When the hospital committee voted against a special ceremony for doctors who had given twenty-five years of service, I celebrated for

myself. I had a gold watch engraved, and commissioned a plaque that reads, DR. HOWARD LIEBGOLD •
KAISER MEDICAL CENTER • 25TH ANNIVERSARY REHABILITATION SERVICES. I went to work wearing a tuxedo
and I felt great.

"When you embrace your death, it frees you. I
was always so concerned about the WPTs and the
ramifications and repercussions of everything I said or
did. Cancer gave me an 'I-don't-give-a-damn' kind of
an attitude after having spent my whole life giving
too much of a damn. When I finally examined my belief system, I changed every rule that didn't work
very well."

The process of healing your phobias can motivate
you to investigate the beliefs and rules that have shaped
your life. When you discard the programs that don't
serve you, you have the opportunity to make new
choices that offer you a personal freedom you may
never have experienced. You may be surprised to discover that you can go beyond your original goal of getting back to where you were before you had panic
attacks. When you can change your beliefs and write
your own rules, you build a new foundation for enjoying the rest of your life.

How About You?

1. Name Your Core Beliefs

Core beliefs are ideas about reality that you hold to be
true. For example, if you believe that one must earn

and pay a high price for every ounce of happiness, your choices will be different than if you believe you are naturally entitled to be happy.

List ten statements that describe your core beliefs *about yourself.* Some examples are: (1) Whatever I do is never good enough. (2) I am a caring person. (3) I have too many emotional needs.

2. Name Your Family Rules

Your family rules are the codes of conduct that were either taught to you directly or were picked up by observing how your family acted. Review different areas of your life, such as finances, work, relationships, body image, love, sex, and spiritual life. Write down your rules on these subjects. (1) I must be careful to control myself or I will be humiliated. (2) I can't spend money on impractical things. (3) Don't wear blue jeans when you go downtown because people will stare at you and know you don't respect yourself. Include even seemingly insignificant things that you were told as a child because they may have a considerable impact on how you see yourself. Through this process you will see how family rules have become your personal rules, and how they may reinforce your core beliefs.

3. Write Your Own Rules

Take each of the *core beliefs* and *family rules* and rewrite it in a way that would be supportive and freeing for you. For example: (1) Acknowledging my feelings and emotional needs is healthy. I can be creative and flexible in finding ways to satisfy these needs. (2) I enjoy many aspects of my life because I can relax and trust myself. (3) I appreciate myself. My self-esteem does not depend on what other people think.

4. Try on New Rules

Choose one of these new rules and try it on. Use your creative imagination to do a success rehearsal. Write a paragraph or speak into a tape player and describe how your life is transformed by this new rule. For example: "I know I can trust myself so I enjoy so many new things. I love going out with friends, but sometimes I just like to be alone. I take a walk or go to a movie by myself. I sit back and laugh and have a good time, and when I go home I feel like I've had a small vacation."

5. Use the Transformation Process

Choose one of your core beliefs and think back to an incident in your childhood that may have reinforced this belief. Use the Transformation Process[1] to identify the core message and then create a new one. Tell the original story out loud *using the present tense.* "I am seven years old and my father yells at me for losing my

---

1. This process was created by Jeru Kabbal, founder of the Institute for Accelerated Personal Transformation. For more information about APT, write P.O. Box 1111, Mill Valley, CA 94942.

book bag . . ." Write down any messages you get or decisions you make as a result of this incident. Then tell the story again, *using the present tense*, intentionally choosing dialogue and behavior that give your child self supportive messages and the opportunity to make new decisions. Write down your new messages and beliefs. Over the next few days, observe your response to the original memory and notice if its effect on you has changed.

11

Can This Really Be Me?

The men and women you have met here will continue to grow and change long after you finish reading this book. Some of them are completely free of panic or phobias. Others, although they sometimes have anxious moments, no longer are consumed by worrying about panic. They are confident that they can take care of themselves if uncomfortable sensations do arise. All have integrated what they have learned into their everyday lives and are fully engaged with the adventure of living. I invite you to allow their progress to inspire and encourage you—wherever you are on your journey to freedom.

Kathy: My World Is Getting Bigger

Several months after Kathy's husband found out that his job was going to be terminated, he was offered a position that required relocating to another state. "When I heard the news, I was scared," said Kathy, "but

even more, I was excited. I immediately said 'Yes.'
Though it was a place I had never been before, I
wholeheartedly decided that I could do whatever was
needed to make the move."

Kathy's biggest challenge was to drive across the
country with her husband to find a place to rent while
they looked for a new home to buy. "After three years
of hardly leaving my house, I was on the road, miles
from home, staying in motels and eating in restaurants.
Of course, I had some uncomfortable moments, but I
got through them. A few months later, when we were
ready to buy a house, our realtor gave us a champagne
dinner at a nice restaurant in town. I was a little nervous about making reservations, but then I reminded
myself that everybody has something to deal with. No
human being on this Earth is perfect or fearless, even if
the things that bother someone else are different from
the things that bother me.

"I don't have as much patience anymore dealing
with my phobia. I want things and I want them now!
Yet I know I'm not a person who can get ahead of
myself. I'm afraid of going too quickly and then having
to go back and start over. So I've taken things kind of
slow, but *I've kept on going.* When something new
comes up, like eating in a fancy restaurant or going
sightseeing, I don't say to myself, 'I'll never do that.' I
may think, 'Not right now, but maybe I'll do that next
month.' I'm feeling good about being able to do a little
more each week. My world is getting bigger.

"Meeting Dr. Liebgold, going to class and talking
to others who have had this problem gave me back my

life. For me it was like living through winter, watching everything die, and then discovering spring again. I was able to look at things differently; everything is new. I enjoy what I get out of each day. Dr. Liebgold taught me more than just how to deal with panic disorder. He helped me love myself. I don't spend my time worrying what people think of me. I've learned to appreciate myself the way I am—a human being who is doing the best I can. When you start relaxing about yourself, you begin to see that all of us are the same; we're all trying to do the best we can. You're not so quick to judge other people, because you realize that you don't know what they've been through in their lives.

"I hate panic, but maybe I am a better person for it. I have learned more about me—how to work for what I want and appreciate what I've got. It feels good to be alive again instead of dead inside. Excitement is replacing dread. It's hard for me to brag about myself, but some days I can look in the mirror and really like who I am."

Brian: Finding His Inner Strength

Over the course of a year, Brian was able to return to work, fly again, travel to Europe, and do everyday tasks without debilitating anxiety. Occasionally Brian had thoughts that he should be more independent, but he and Jim enjoyed being together and everything was going well. "I remember walking one day and thinking I had the perfect life. Jim and I had an almost perfect relationship, we had the perfect dog and the perfect car. But then something grabbed me. It wasn't perfect. Jim had HIV."

Soon after moving into their new house, Jim started experiencing some active symptoms of AIDS. After three months, he was too weak to get out of bed. "I felt so helpless when he lost his appetite and I couldn't do anything about it. I made myself completely available to him, emotionally and physically. I learned how to flush and change IVs; I bathed him; I emptied bedpans. I thought I did pretty well instinctively, for someone who had never done anything like that before."

Brian prepared himself for a long period of caregiving at home, but Jim had to be moved to the hospital because his liver was not functioning properly. Brian spent many days and nights at Jim's bedside, until finally a friend gently urged him to go home and get some rest. At 4:59 that morning, Brian woke up sensing that Jim was saying good-bye to him. A few minutes later, the phone rang and Brian was told that Jim had passed away.

Brian feels that his exploration with his phobia therapist gave him some resources to face this traumatic loss. "The experience with panic forced me to open up some old wounds from earlier in my life. It helped me recognize the emotional isolation I felt growing up, and examine the terrible fear of separation I had when I was away from Jim. For much of my life, I was uncomfortable just being on this planet. I couldn't see any reason why I should be so unhappy or why I should live the rest of my life like that. Through healing my fear of panic, I made peace with being alive and living more in the present."

Several weeks after Jim's death, Brian returned to work. "I have no regrets about my relationship with him. I loved him and know that he loved me. I grieve every day. The mornings are awful. But the whole day isn't, and some moments are fine. When I start to think ahead and wonder if I can stand always being this sad, I remember not to project into the future. And little things that seemed like such a problem are not a big deal anymore. I go out and do what I need to. I drive all over by myself. I haven't once thought of taking a drink; I have thought of smoking but haven't done it. I haven't used medication. I have intense feelings, but know I can get through this."

Brian made plans to take a trip later in the year. "I've been through so much. I've received so much support from so many people, but now I am ready to get away by myself, to an entirely new place where Jim and I have never been. I did some research and found a bed and breakfast inn in Cape Cod where they serve a real breakfast—pancakes, oatmeal, omelettes. I'm a breakfast man. When Jim and I were in Europe, I never could get used to the continental breakfast. When I made my reservation, I told myself, 'If I don't like being there, I can leave. I'll know what's right for me.'"

Alicia: Sincere Meaning

When Alicia resigned from her last job, she didn't know what she would do in the future. She longed to find something she could really care about. "Of course, I would love to feel 'normal' all the time, but I don't. I can't put my life on hold until everything is perfect, so I choose to put my attention on what has sincere meaning for me and move in that direction.

"Going to school again is my therapy. It's getting easier since I no longer feel so bound by other people's expectations or my interpretation of them. I always try to raise my hand and speak in class. When I turn in some work, I don't worry about it so much. I have become more accepting of myself; I know that whatever I do each day is my best, and I don't tell myself it should be better. In the last year, I've attended night classes and weekend seminars and have gone out to lunch with other students I didn't even know very well. I could never have done these things a year ago. I'm happy with what I am and who I am now.

"The greatest thing for me is when I can do something so unselfconsciously that I don't have to think about it. For example, I discovered what I thought was an error in my bank statement, so I went down to the bank on Saturday. The woman at the desk didn't want to take the time to help me, so she told me to come back Monday. 'I'll be happy to come back Monday,' I agreed, 'but then I need an appointment with someone.' She mumbled under her breath and it was clear she didn't want to do that either. Finally, she said, 'Okay, I'll take care of you now.' She was sitting and I was standing at the counter, so I asked, 'Do you suppose we could both sit down?' I waited, and eventually she took me to a desk where we both could sit.

"Before she even looked at my statement, she told me that the computer never makes mistakes. I said, 'Yes, but we all know who programs the computers, don't we?'

So we went over the statement, and in a few minutes we found out it was my error. I thanked her for her time and said, 'That was great. All I wanted to know was where the problem was. I feel so much better.' And I honestly meant it. I felt good about being assertive and saying the things I did. I didn't get angry, I didn't get upset, I didn't get anxious. When I walked out, I thought, 'Do you know what you just did? You spoke out, you were wonderful—and you didn't even think twice about doing it.' It felt natural to be confident and assertive. I relish those moments. I am having more and more of them."

Claire: Awakening from Panic

At first glance, nothing is radically different in Claire's life. She is still married to Ray. She still works at the same job. But from her vantage point, everything is different. Naming her condition was once an essential part of her healing journey, but today she no longer identifies herself as phobic. "Panic was a passage, not a stopping place. I learned from panic how to listen to myself.

"A few months ago I had a dream. I was climbing a granite wall that was sheer vertical. I could feel the sun on my back and my fingers hooking into crevices. I was intent on what I was doing, and then a taunting voice said, 'You're climbing a mountain. You can't do that, you have panic.' Then a second voice joined in and said, 'You don't have that anymore; we *can* do this.' It was an incredible experience to see myself keep climbing up. And you know, I reached the top! I climbed that mountain. I woke up feeling so full. I felt big inside.

"When I was severely phobic, I didn't realize how time-consuming my fear was. I spent hours thinking about how to make excuses or calling hotels to find out what alternatives I had to using the elevator. Making plans to avoid my fear consumed all of me. Once I became free of my fear of panic, I discovered all this extra time. I'm even taking a Spanish class after work so I can communicate better with Spanish-speaking clients.

"I am awakening from panic because I am living fully right now. I'm in touch with my wants, desires, and passions. Now I have many choices. I can get myself food without waiting for someone to go to the store for me or with me. When I hear there's a sale on underwear, I can go by myself and get what I want. I have the freedom to go to sleep at night and be relaxed, without worrying that I'll bolt out of bed in terror. I have the freedom to change my mind, to say 'no,' to be me. I don't have to change myself to please other people. I am free to give to myself and others.

"To someone else, I may appear the same, but life is so different now. It's vivid. I'm smelling and hearing and tasting and touching and seeing and feeling everything in such a new way. I'm getting so much pleasure from the thing I feared most—life!"

Bonnie: Having Choices

"It's great to be free of that constant anxiety I used to live with. I can't really describe this new feeling or praise it highly enough. Back when I was suffering, I couldn't have imagined a day when I didn't think about panic all the time. It took up most of my waking hours. Now I'm happy to have my daughter taking up my time.

"After graduating from the university, I wanted to go on to teaching, but first I concentrated on using the cassette home study program to free myself from panic. Later I took a very demanding position teaching elementary school. I never could have done it without the tools I learned to reduce anxiety. The job was stressful, but I didn't react to the stress as I would have in the past.

"I know I always have choices. I choose to stay home to raise my baby, but I'm not housebound. This time is so different from the years when I kept my anxiety a secret and I tried to handle everything alone and look so perfect. I've come a long way in being assertive in my marriage and in other relationships. I am able to feel my feelings.

"At this point, I really don't think much about panic or phobia. The process of healing did bring up important issues for me to look at, like how I fit into the world and how I see myself connected to other people. It helped me clear up some traumas from childhood. But panic is not in the forefront for me anymore. I'm glad to put it behind me and learn from other things.

"I see myself raising an open, loving child who feels secure and able to express whatever she's feeling or what she needs or desires. I want to give her what I never had as a child—freedom from shoulds and expectations that are unrealistic. I am teaching her to trust herself, as I am finally learning to trust myself."

Howard: Free to Serve, Free to Have Fun

"I have been freed from the jail of fear and I am able to do virtually anything I wish. I still have occasional phobic thoughts, but I don't let them escalate. Last year I took a bus tour through Europe. The first thing the tour director said when we got on the bus was, 'Welcome. We are all going to be together on this bus for fifteen days.' I never get on a bus without remembering that for thirty years I couldn't do that. I've been on fifty bus trips in countries throughout the world, and every time it's almost like a religious experience. I hear a voice in me saying, 'Thank you. I'm here because I have been able to overcome that fear of panic.'"

Howard is ready to retire from his position in the rehabilitation department, but his plan after retirement is to continue his work with people who have anxiety disorders. "I've realized lately that what I love the most is teaching, especially because I know that I am saving lives. My older son committed suicide many years before I learned that phobias and panic attacks could be cured. No one made the right diagnosis. It was only later, after I got educated about panic, that I looked back and said, 'Oh my God, now I know what he had.' I've dealt with the reality and the frustration that at that time in my life I didn't have the knowledge to give him what he needed.

"But his death is certainly one of the motivating forces for continuing to teach. It gives me the greatest satisfaction to take a call from a person who is ready to give up and be able to tell them, 'Listen, what you have is curable. You don't believe it, do you? I'm telling you right now, because I'm a cocky rascal and I've been there.'

"I understand now that for thirty-one years I wasn't fooling around. I was training to be a world's expert on panic as a result of my own experience. I've been able to help thousands of other people, even though I couldn't do that for my own son.

"But I'm not leaving a seventy-hour-a-week job for an eighty-hour-a-week job. I also see myself playing—tennis, fishing, dancing, traveling. Fortunately, there's a part of me that's never grown up, so you can bet I'm going to keep having fun."

Edward: Living in a Technicolor World

"I never thought I could have a family. I believed I was too phobic to take kids to a football game or attend a P.T.A. meeting. I envisioned a bleak existence for the rest of my life—alone, not necessarily housebound, but limited to an area maybe five miles square. After I got into the TERRAP phobia class and then the twelve-step program, I was able to go to Hawaii and Mexico and begin a long-term committed relationship with Judy. We began to talk about possibilities I had never expected, like having kids. Recently, I took my two daughters on a four-hundred-mile car trip to Disneyland. If you had asked me ten years ago if these things were possible, I would have said you were hallucinating. My world has gone from black and white to technicolor.

"My wife has been disabled by a neuromuscular illness, so I handle most of the physical care of our daughters. Often I am so busy doing what is needed that I can't stop to think whether or not I have butter-flies in my stomach. When I do have a moment to reflect back, I realize that I've been functioning without questioning my ability or self-control. I've started to trust that I can cope when I need to. I've begun to have a different image of myself both at home and at work. I belong to several professional organizations for which I volunteer when I can. This year at the awards dinner, I was given a plaque for being member of the year. I was astounded. It never occurred to me that the little things I do are so appreciated.

"Looking back at my struggle with panic and pho-bia, I see it as a crucible that tempered me and helped me grow. I beat myself up for too many years before I understood that my phobias are physical responses that I can manage with a positive mental attitude, appropri-ate self-disclosure, some twelve-step support, relax-ation, and a little love and help from friends. I feel that my condition has helped me become what I am today."

Mani: Journey to India

In November 1992, I went to India for five weeks. That is a long way to go for someone who once couldn't fly from

San Francisco to Los Angeles or drive the fifteen miles to work. But the distance wasn't just geographical; it reflected how far I have traveled on my healing journey.

For many years I had dreamed of going to India. In college I took courses in Indian art and was entranced by the rhythms of Indian ragas. In my search for meaning, I have been drawn to Eastern philosophies and traditions. But when I became phobic about flying, I gave up all hope of ever fulfilling my dream. In 1992, an old friend returned from a trip to northern India and told me about a teacher named Sri Poonja (respectfully called Papaji by people who know him). She described her experience of sitting with him and listening to him, and having a realization of her true nature. She was no longer ruled by her emotional ups and downs or thrown into a panic by her thoughts. "The inner struggle against myself is over," my friend told me. "I know who I am in a way that can't be lost no matter what I do or don't do. I no longer need to be anything other than what I am or where I am at this moment. This is freedom." Looking into her eyes, I sensed a calm joy. To my amazement, a voice inside me said, "Yes! I'd like to meet this person you describe and I'm *ready* to go to India!"

Within moments, all my questions and considerations came up. I hadn't traveled in a foreign country for almost thirty years. I was in the middle of writing this book. What if I got sick? What if . . . ? Then I remembered the sign on the table in Howard Liebgold's phobia class: *Comfort Is Not Our Goal, Living Is.* In the ten years since I had started healing from panic, I had learned more about my mind and body than I had ever known before. Now I had the motivation and the tools. Whatever came up, I was prepared to take care of myself.

In the months that followed, I had neither time nor energy for fear rehearsals; instead I channeled my adrenalin into the excitement of making plane reservations and phone calls to arrange the trip for Michael and me. On November 5, 1992, we boarded a jumbo jet and embarked on our journey into unknown territory. As the plane picked up speed, I closed my eyes and whispered to myself, "Breathing in, I calm my body and my mind. Breathing out, I feel alive."

The eighteen-hour flight was tiring but easy. On the other hand, traveling in India *was* sometimes difficult. Knowing that the hygienic standards for food and water in Asia were different than in the West made me nervous about eating. Although I minimized the risks by getting sensible information from others who had been there, for the first day I had a phobic fear of eating; I dreaded the time when I would run out of the snacks I had pocketed on the airplane. At breakfast the second morning, I watched Michael devour toast, a soft-boiled egg, and a cup of coffee without dropping dead. I took a deep breath, said a prayer, and ordered a meal. It tasted delicious!

I worried about having an accident or getting lost. I was especially afraid of racing through traffic in the bicycle-drawn rickshaws. But I knew I couldn't afford to dwell on these fears. STOP! *Count 1-2-3-4. I can handle it.* I brought my attention back to what was in front of me and asked myself, "Is there any problem right now?" The answer was usually "No!" Once, however, when I thought that the rickshaw driver was going to race his bicycle in front of the oncoming traffic, I grabbed the back of his shirt and stopped him in his tracks. I decided to get off and walk. After a while, I realized that I always had choices, even far from home. Wherever I was, I could just be myself.

I did many things that were new for me. I walked across the Ganges on a narrow footbridge. I had a shopping bag full of bananas torn out of my hands by a pack of neighborhood monkeys. I posed for pictures in front of the Taj Mahal. I laughed with Papaji, sang him a song, and gave him a hug. But most important of all, I discovered that the secret to the freedom I had been seeking was already mine. The very core of what made this man so alive, so joyful, so genuine, was essentially not different from what I had been learning all along in healing from panic and phobias: *Relax the body. Relax the mind. Don't live in the memories of the past (no matter what happened last time or five minutes ago). Don't anticipate the future with fear rehearsals. When fear thoughts arise, watch them come, let them go. Relax and come back to what is here and now.*

I realized that my experience of healing from panic and phobias had not been a detour on my journey—it was at the very heart of my spiritual path. I had gone halfway around the world to discover that freedom is my choice to stay in the present moment and my willingness to accept myself. Nothing, not even panic, can take that away.

How About You?

Write Your Own "Can This Really Be Me?" Letter

Take a few minutes to relax your body. Then close your eyes and imagine all the things you would love to be doing in the next two years. Don't put any limits on your visions. Next, move ahead to a time two years from now, and write a letter to a friend describing your gratitude and awe at what has transpired in your life. Write about everything you've dreamed of as though it has already happened. Breathe deeply and feel your gratitude and amazement as you write.

For example, I might write something like this: "Dear Loie, I've just returned from touring Europe to celebrate my book being published in German, French, and Italian. I am so touched by the people who have chauffeured me around and shown me such hospitality . . ." Write at least two pages, describing your remarkable healing and freedom in great detail. Plant the seed that can grow in your life.

12

Trusting
Life

I sent everyone I knew postcards from India—pictures of the crowded streets of Delhi, the temples along the Ganges at Rishikesh, and the marketplace at the foot of the Himalayan mountains. When I returned from traveling, friends who had known me through the years of panic and isolation were amazed. "That's great," one of them marveled, "I guess you're cured forever." I appreciated her enthusiasm but told her I couldn't anticipate forever. "I don't worry about panic anymore," I said, "because now I have the tools to take care of myself." Our conversation gave me the opportunity to realize how much I had grown.

Panic had turned my life in a new direction by forcing me to investigate the lens through which I viewed all my experiences. Ever since my father's death, my perspective had been shaped by anticipation of loss or separation. The cultural and religious traditions of my childhood did not provide either an emotional or spiritual context to help me understand and master my fears. Gradually I internalized the belief that

I was a helpless individual fighting alone to survive against constant threats in a frightening world. I sometimes thought of other people as the enemy who might find out that I was inadequate or less than what I claimed to be.

As I became an adult, my hope for security was to gain control—of myself, of others, of outside circumstances. When panic interfered with my plan, I condemned myself as inadequate. It didn't occur to me that my *strategy* might be the problem. Nor did I see the connection between my bouts of fear and my beliefs about life. As I pieced together the puzzle of my history, I began to understand that not only had I stopped trusting myself, I had stopped trusting life. The discoveries I made while healing from panic transformed my life view and gave me back the ability to trust.

From Separation to Trust

My trust grew in increments, bolstered by tangible, definable acts, such as driving one more exit on the freeway or taking an elevator to the tenth floor. My trust expanded with the experience of gratitude each time I endured the symptoms of panic and nothing terrible happened; each time a friend understood me or a stranger was helpful; each time life gave me just what I needed.

My trust is not an abstract concept or a form of magical thinking. It has evolved out of actual experiences that occurred on all levels—physical, mental, emotional, and spiritual: I have proven to my satisfaction that uncomfortable sensations won't kill me or make me crazy. I know what stimulates adrenalin and what reduces it, and I have a track record of victories to assure me that my tools work. I understand that my exaggerated fear of being alone or separated from safety is related to my childhood feelings of loss or abandonment. And I have developed a deep trust in a divine presence, or higher power, which is always with me and part of me.

If the old, familiar feeling of aloneness arises, I remind myself that although the feeling is real, it does not signal a real danger. I can get back my equilibrium by drawing upon my memory of people who have cared about me or touched me in some way. Even if they are not physically with me, remembering them often comforts me.

My trust has been strengthened by all the small incidents that show me that life does have a supportive intelligence: getting a table at my favorite restaurant on my birthday because the maitre d' got a cancellation just as my husband and I walked in the door, or a woman pulling over when I had a flat tire and offering her car phone to call road service. These events no longer seem coincidental; they all confirm a *new* story: that life really does support and care for all of us. This belief allows me to feel related to all people without feeling responsible for them. I no longer try to run the world, so I am willing to be "in charge" of whatever is in my domain—my breathing, my communication, my driving.

I have a relationship to a spiritual source, or higher power. This relationship is not confined to a cathedral or meditation hall. It is always available to me. When I look over at the other cars on the highway, instead of telling myself that I am alone and surrounded by strangers, I say to myself, "These people are not separate from me. They are not my enemies or judges. They are just me in another form. We are all sharing a moment together here in the natural flow of life." Or I assure myself, "The presence of God spirit is with me here, as everywhere. I am perfectly cared for. All is well."

As I interviewed people for the last time, I asked them if their healing process had been linked to a deepening spirituality. Several described their spiritual growth as an increasing trust in themselves, in their connection to other human beings, and in a spiritual presence.

Reaching Out and Letting Go

For Alicia, developing trust began with reaching out to other people as well as consciously developing her own practice of prayer and meditation. "Particularly in light of my social phobia, I have had to discover from my own experience that if I open myself to other people, they are usually caring and understanding. No one's been shocked when I've told them that I have panic disorder or when I've talked about my fears of being alone. Of course, once I feel accepted, I feel less alone."

A recent experience illustrates how a shift in Alicia's perception changed her relationship to others: "I had to go to a weekend psychology seminar that included some experiential processes and exercises with the other participants. This is challenging for me to begin with, but to make matters worse, when I checked my schedule at the last minute, I discovered that I hadn't done the required reading. So I went to class on Saturday completely unprepared. I had some of the old thoughts about being exposed, and I felt isolated from the other students.

"The day wasn't easy, but I managed to stay for the whole class. I even admitted how I was feeling. I talked about the sense of aloneness that sometimes terrifies me, in spite of having a loving family and friends. That evening, just before going to sleep, I took a few minutes to relax in meditation, which I do every night to clear my mind. As I became calm, a visual image appeared. I saw clouds, and behind them a brilliant sun peeking out like a half circle of golden light. I thought, 'There's your answer. There will be clouds in your life, but the sun is always there behind them; God is always there. Sometimes you have to trust your connection and look to your heart to feel it.' The image was so beautiful and it made me feel warm and relaxed. Then, just as I was about to fall off asleep, I heard a voice that sounded like a woman whispering in my ear, saying, 'It's okay.' I'd never before had any auditory experience in my meditations. Astonished, I opened my eyes, then settled back into the feeling of warmth and connectedness to something larger than myself. It was such a peaceful and reassuring voice.

"Driving to class the next day, I felt like I was seeing the world with new eyes. Colors were richer and
clearer. I wasn't afraid and I didn't feel alone. I felt in
touch with myself, connected with the other people, and
in turn felt a deeper relatedness with the Earth, with
spirituality, with everything that is inherently part of us.

"I can still call upon what I experienced in that
meditative state, what it looked and felt like. I can
recapture that feeling by being open to other people.
Part of my continuing learning is to recognize what I do
have control over and what I don't. It's a relief that I
can surrender my worry to a higher source and trust
that everything is okay. I often say a prayer that my
grandmother taught me when I was a child. It brings
me back to that feeling of being comforted. 'The Light
of God surrounds me; The Love of God enfolds me;
The Power of God protects me; The Presence of God
watches over me; Wherever I am, God is.'"

Serenity

Through the TERRAP phobia program, Edward began
to feel that other people understood him, but he didn't
relate his healing process to spiritual growth until he
went to A.A. "Having panic and trying to cover it by
using alcohol had isolated me from others. Except
when I was an eight-year-old in a buddy-based gang, I
don't think I have had any sense of belonging with people. I remember the first time I had a real sense of a
spiritual presence that made me feel included in something bigger. It was at the close of an A.A. meeting. We

were standing in a circle, holding hands and saying the Lord's Prayer. I got a ninety-second rush—I felt genuinely connected to the other people in the circle, as well as to a higher power.

"At first I had that feeling of peace and oneness only in the meetings. Then, several months later, I had the same feeling sitting at home in my easy chair. I could see the sun just above the window, and the sunbeams were falling across the room in a certain way. It's not like the heavens opened up and angels came down with a sign that said, 'This is the moment.' It wasn't anything that dramatic. But I just relaxed mentally and I felt part of a larger peace. I found myself thinking, 'This is serenity.'

"At the same time, my work with panic was really changing my life. Just being mobile opened up new possibilities. When you're phobic you can't drive to the seacoast alone, so you rarely get to enjoy the panorama of nature. When you start to recover, you can go to the beach by yourself and look up at the sky and say to yourself, 'This is a big world and somebody made this.' When I was able to start driving on my own, go hiking again, and be in nature away from everybody else, I realized that there's an organizing principle here—it's a bigger world than just my problems, and I am part of that bigger reality.

"I've heard it said that God doesn't give you more than you can handle. I didn't believe that until I got to know myself enough to discover what was already there—enough brain power, enough muscle power, even enough soul power. I didn't need more than I already had. All I needed was a different way of thinking. This doesn't apply just to phobias or staying sober. It changes the way I approach everything in my life.

"The days that are most meaningful to me are not the sunny, bright ones when everyone is playing on the beach. On the stormy days when the waves are whipping up, I get a sense that there are seasons, that the world revolves. I don't have to fix myself today. I can take some time in this learning process. If I don't feel a lot of serenity today, there will be more tomorrow. I don't have to get it all right at once."

"Us"ness

Claire created her own definition of freedom the night she went to hear a popular author without bringing her "weapons." Her husband had to work that night, so he dropped her off at the auditorium and arranged to pick her up at the end of the evening. "I found myself sitting in a hot, crowded room, surrounded by complete strangers. As I was waiting for the program to begin, I realized I didn't have a watch, the key to my house, my purse, my ID, money, or any of the things I used to think I needed *in case* something happened to me. I can't say that I intentionally planned to not bring anything, but when I noticed that my hands were empty, I realized I didn't need any 'weapons' to protect myself. I didn't need them because I didn't see myself as separate from everyone else. I sat there trusting the feeling of 'us'ness; I felt free.

"Before I was able to trust *us,* I had to trust myself. Panic showed me that I had broken trust with myself. Building trust with myself was a step-by-step process. It meant making agreements with myself and giving myself permission to change my mind. It grew from taking small risks, like touching the elevator and taking one step inside. It came from grabbing the hand of my child self and saying, 'It's okay to feel everything you feel, but I am going to be the adult and I am going to ask you to trust me. I won't force you or do anything that will hurt you.'

"Then it shifted to another phase. Once I created the trust, it opened the way to finding that this feeling of trust is not just limited to me. My trust means: I trust you and I trust my experience with life and I trust this moment right now. I don't need to 'awfulize' the future. I trust that it is also safe for me to express all of who I am—my anger, my sadness, my happiness. I'm more than any one feeling.

"Recently I had my wisdom teeth pulled, something that needed to be done for fifteen years. I was afraid. It wasn't panic, it was healthy fear. As they put an IV in me and hooked me up to an EKG machine, I turned to the assistant and said, 'I'm afraid.' She nodded and said, 'I understand.' And then I had the profound feeling of being safe. I thought, 'I'm with people I've just met; I'm about to lose consciousness. I don't know what's going to happen and this is wonderful.' I started to repeat, 'I am here with me, I am here with me,' and the words became, 'My dentist and Mary are

here with me, we are here.' The next thing I remember
is waking up and knowing I was safe, even though I had
been medicated, and was in a tall building in a big city.
I was able to trust people I didn't know very well.

"Trust grows from my understanding that I am not
alone. I am part of something spectacular. For example,
even baking bread becomes a spiritual experience for
me. Kneading the bread, I remember doing the same
thing with my mother. Simultaneously I know that I am
going to be sharing that bread with someone else. The
inclusiveness goes further, to the point of understanding all the other things that went into this moment of
kneading dough. Where did the flour come from?
Where did the water come from to make the wheat
grow? Who ground the wheat into flour and delivered it
to the store? All of a sudden it's not just a loaf of bread.
It's an understanding that I am not alone in this world."

Finding Peace with Himself

At the height of Brian's crisis with panic, his greatest
fear was being separated from Jim. Now, after Jim's
death, he *is* on his own, and often gets tired of having
to make so many decisions by himself. At the same
time, Brian has experienced a profound realization that
he isn't ever alone. "When I was growing up, I felt different, like I didn't belong. I saw the world as a mine-
field that I had to negotiate by myself. My phobic feelings were like that too; I thought that the world was a
dangerous place. I remember drinking and doing drugs

when I was young just to escape those feelings. Now I reach out to people by being honest about myself, and I put my trust in God.

"Many people discover their connection to a higher power when they're at a low point in their lives. I make my connection consciously on a daily basis. I ask for God's support to help me get through whatever is in front of me and to help me move on to whatever is next. I try to remember to thank Him first.

"Even though I have suffered such deep loss, I don't feel like I'm alone. I feel Jim's presence, and I don't know or care where his presence leaves off and God's begins. Sometimes I get caught up in my own worries and forget the connection; then something reminds me that I am always cared for. I had an experience of this one day while walking down the street on my way to work. I was overwhelmed by a feeling of terror. I knew I wasn't worried about going to work or being on the street; I was just terrified about the unknown future looming ahead of me. Then I felt Jim's arm rest on my shoulder, assuring me that everything was going to be okay. I knew he was around to help me through this. In that moment, I relaxed. I just let go."

Brian no longer focuses on panic as a major issue in his life, but he values the things he learned from his experience with it. "Before I educated myself about anxiety and panic, I was so afraid and confused. I resented feeling so uncomfortable on my own planet. But trying to change the world or control my feelings never worked for me, and it's not where I focus my attention now. At times I wish that I was over my grief, but I don't fight myself. Whether I feel fear or sadness, I don't grit my teeth and force my way through it. I just stop whatever I'm doing and take a walk or relax. What matters to me is peace with myself.

"It really has helped to talk to other people and find out that they also have major dysfunctions or limitations. Everyone has something. No one has a free ticket or a smooth ride all their life, even if they look like they've got everything. We're all in this boat together, whether we have anxiety or not. I've got mine and you've got yours.

"Very good people have been put into my life, and now I know I don't have to do everything or solve everything by myself. I'm very healthy, and I want to be happy and enjoy life. I feel like I'll probably be on this planet for quite a while."

Trusting the Present Moment

We often use the word *trust* to refer to our hope that some future expectation will be fulfilled. But trust in the future can only develop from trust in the present moment. In order to reduce our adrenalin, we practice keeping our minds from drifting to past failures or future fear rehearsals. We learn to keep our attention focused on what is present in our environment. The same kind of focus on what is here and now can guide us to experience trust, not just to handle our fears but to experience the fullness and richness of life.

Cured of his claustrophobia and free of cancer, Howard resolved to savor each moment of living. "I attended a seminar that began with the leader turning over an hourglass. She said to us, 'You can't do anything about the sand that's already fallen—that's the past. You can't do anything about the sand that hasn't fallen yet—that's the future.' Watching that hourglass the whole day, I understood that my happiness is directly related to how I choose to experience the grains of sand going through at any given moment.

"Knowing how affected I was by that perception, my wife bought me a two-and-a-half-foot-high hourglass for my birthday. I start each day by turning the hourglass over; that's my reminder to live fully, to not let my precious sand slip by unnoticed. I wake up each morning with gratitude for being alive. I give thanks for what works and what *isn't* a problem today. When I go for a walk, I don't just go on a walk to get somewhere or to get exercise. I smell the air, look at the flowers, and acknowledge, 'You're here now, you're alive.'

"I learned that relishing a day is not something that happens by accident. I thank God, myself, and other human beings that I have been freed of so much baggage from the past and am able to genuinely love life."

Living in the present does not mean ignoring responsibilities or plans for the future. But the present moment is the channel through which all energy enters our lives; it is the ground for all creative possibilities. You may not always enjoy what is happening in the present moment, especially if you are preoccupied with anticipating future disappointments or are impatient for something else to happen. In reality, most of the suffering that we believe comes from our immediate circumstances is actually caused by the *interpretation* we create about it in our minds. If you use your senses and open your eyes to what is here and now, you may discover that each moment offers a new experience with its own unique flavor and fulfillment. This moment is the gateway to creating the next.

I remember a comment made by a woman I met many years ago. She told me of a moment in which she experienced the blessings of her life, even though she was having difficulties with panic. "I was in my back yard having a barbecue dinner with my family. Out of the blue, a calm came over me and I had a feeling of complete fulfillment. It was as if I had taken my worrying self out of the picture. It was very fleeting, just one moment in time. I looked down and saw . . . everything was perfect. I felt so peaceful, I wished that it could continue like that forever. It doesn't, but just being aware of those moments makes everything else seem lighter. I can look around and say, 'It's pretty good.'"

Trust can't be manufactured, but its presence can be nurtured. It grows if you remember to stop for a sunset or watch the seagulls soar. It becomes stronger when you look at the bigger panorama beyond your immediate needs and problems and know that the clouds will pass. Respect your connection to all other living beings and listen to the wisdom of your heart and your soul. Honor a vision of the greater whole while letting yourself experience the fullness of the present moment. You may discover that the cycle of discovery initiated by fear will lead to a renewal of trust—in yourself, in others, and in the infinite, caring nature of life.

How About You?

1. Enjoy the Present Moment

Designate a signal to remind you to pay attention to the present moment. You can set your watch alarm to go off at regular intervals, or reserve a moment before you begin each meal. At the given signal, stop whatever you are doing, thinking, or saying and become aware of the present. Notice your breath, the colors and textures around you, the physical sensations in your body. If you wish, you can whisper to yourself, "Breathing in, I feel myself breathing in; breathing out, I see the red telephone."

2. Keep a Trust Log

Set aside a section in your journal to record instances and events that remind you to trust the synchronicity of life. Whenever you are blessed with "things just coming together," or an experience in which a person you wanted or needed to reach "just showed up," or a situation that occurred at the right time, make a note in your journal so you can begin to notice the correlation among seemingly random events. For example:

1/7/95   *I was talking to the woman next to me at the gym and found out that she had edited many books. She offered to take a look at my book and give me some feedback.*

1/20/95   *For the last few days I've found myself thinking about my old friend JoAnne. I haven't heard from her in years. I went to the mailbox today and found a letter from her.*

Does looking back at your entries help you feel that you can trust life?

13

Your Journey

Congratulations! You've taken the time to look at what may be one of the most difficult issues in your life. You have had the courage to examine your fears and to listen with an open mind to some of the choices available to you. You may even feel intuitively that your struggle with anxiety is a hurdle and at the same time an opportunity. In the Sufi tradition there is a saying: "The rose is beautiful, but bless the thorn." This challenge may be the thorn that propels you on your journey to freedom. Even fear can be an invitation to awaken and discover who you are.

Find Out What Works for You

Many of us found that our healing process took us far beyond our original goal of being able to manage our anxiety. But no matter where our journey led us, we all started with the basics—learning to relax the body, transform anxiety-producing thoughts, and reduce adrenalin. Though aspects of your situation may be unique, you can build the foundation of your program on the basic principles that have been used effectively by many other people. Brian once thought that seeking help was pointless because no one would be able to relate to his experiences. He now says, "No one has to continue living in such extreme discomfort. There are so many proven avenues that you can choose to learn how to take care of yourself." There's no reason to undermine your healing by imagining that you are the one person for whom the tools won't work.

Use the techniques that have been helpful for other people as guidelines. Adapt them to your style of learning. Take what you need. The rest is there waiting if you wish to explore it in the future. Don't give up if one tool or method doesn't seem to help you immediately. Ask yourself if you've been consistent or given it enough time. Some people move slowly and steadily, others make progress in leaps and spurts. It takes time to adapt and incorporate new information and new behavior into your life. Howard told me, "After working with over six thousand patients, I truly believe that panic disorders and phobias are absolutely, unequivocally curable. The most important thing is to make a commitment and don't stop. Face your fear correctly and it will truly disappear."

Cultivate Motivation

Where does the motivation to heal come from? Sometimes it comes from feeling desperate. You'll try something new because you are too miserable staying where you are. Once you get started, motivation often comes from the satisfaction of seeing your own progress. When you believe you can be free, you are more willing to prepare yourself for the things that matter to you.

If you've been frustrated or discouraged for a long time, you may need to cultivate motivation until your innate enthusiasm returns. Motivation can be stimulated with a mixture of discipline, patience, and trust. I observed this chemistry watching my former husband, who is an artist. He didn't wait for inspiration to come. Each day he prepared his materials, and whether or not he was in the mood to paint, he worked with whatever came to him. He took risks and didn't always get the results he expected, but his commitment was to a larger process of expression. He was often more inspired after a day of work than before he started. Creative breakthroughs came with commitment and hard work.

I see a parallel with facing fear. You begin by doing the next appropriate step—whatever task or action you have selected. Edward says, "Perfection is not really necessary, just little incremental pieces of progress." Motivation grows when you regard all your experiences with respect. You know how much courage it took for you to take a step that might have seemed ordinary to someone who doesn't understand panic. You have an opportunity to rekindle the appreciation that comes from within you and can't be taken away by someone else. Kathy believes, "Everything counts. All those little steps add up to something bigger. Don't expect so much of yourself, just see what happens." If you become impatient because you want to do everything immediately, consider it a healthy sign that your motivation is coming back. You can turn your eagerness into a success rehearsal.

Each small action is a building block for something that has meaning and value for you. The desire to go to Europe with Jim helped motivate Brian to overcome his fear of flying. Alicia's faith that she had something worthwhile to contribute to others kept her in school even though it meant she had to confront her anxiety. Evaluate what really matters to you. Your ideas of what would be fulfilling for you may be different from what they were ten years ago. Redefining what is important to you can liberate energy that has been directed toward goals that are no longer priorities for you.

In the midst of crisis, you may worry that you won't have the time or opportunity to fulfill your dreams. Even facing the reality that you're going to die someday can be a positive, motivating force. When my friend Luke was terminally ill with cancer, I learned from him to appreciate the preciousness of each day. As his limitations became more pronounced, he seemed to derive greater satisfaction from even small things—the taste of Halloween candies, the sound of a bird singing outside his window, the ability to sit on the living room couch and visit with friends. He reminded me to be grateful for my options in spite of having problems. His attitude was not a denial of his pain, or mine. It was a reflection of his ability to cherish life.

Don't allow a preoccupation with your limits to blind you to the richness that is available at any moment. You don't need to postpone your life until you get past current obstacles. Savor the things that warm your heart and make you laugh. Make time for activities that bring vital energy to your body, like walking in nature or dancing. When you engage yourself with what is available to you right now, you will have more motivation to pursue your long-term goals.

Welcome Your Emerging Self

In order to grow, you sometimes have to leave behind a familiar way of being before you are sure of what will replace it. Old ways of coping with fear have insulated you like a cocoon. But the strategies that once seemed like a protection don't leave enough room to grow. It takes courage to give up familiar habits, even those that cause pain. It takes trust to allow something new and unknown to emerge. Claire once told me that she didn't know what kind of person she would be without panic. "I knew how to control panic to a degree. I knew how to live with panic. I didn't know how to live *without* it. I didn't know what qualities I would need for this new way of being."

Healing does not mean that you lose the right to ask for emotional or practical support. I met a woman whose husband carried a beeper when she was severely phobic so she could reach him at any moment. "Now that I am better," she told me, "he doesn't carry his beeper anymore. I felt some loss at first because even though I hated being so phobic, I missed the emotional support. Now I'm starting to find new ways to experience intimacy with him. I don't control him, but I still have genuine needs and wants." You don't have to *need* someone in order to justify asking for attention or engagement.

The people you have met here went through a broad process of transformation, which included changing attitudes and beliefs in order to find a new freedom. Released from the burden of having to be perfect, Bonnie was able to give herself the permission to make choices. As Kathy began to appreciate and respect herself, she experienced a renewal of self-esteem and creativity. Edward found that recovering from panic also meant a renewal of self-confidence and recognition of his wholeness. Listening to herself with compassion has given Claire a sense of being intensely alive and engaged with the present moment. Curing his phobias led Howard toward fulfilling his life purpose of saving lives by teaching others how to face their fear. Alicia experienced a deepening trust in herself and in a spiritual presence. Brian used his work with fear as preparation for a major life transition and as a catalyst for developing a sense of belonging and connection to others.

When I was accustomed to living with chronic worry, I did not realize how much of my creative energy and passion for life was being channeled into the service of my anxiety. Panic forced me to take time and energy to know myself better. It enabled me to remember a child who felt emotionally wounded. It made me aware of the spiritual sustenance I had longed for but couldn't name. By showing me how to renew trust in myself, it helped me discover a connection to the sacredness of life.

Often the changes set in motion by panic continue to evolve, long after the initial crisis has passed. When you emerge from your cocoon and start to fly with new wings, you don't turn into somebody else. You become more fully who you already are.

The Discovery of Freedom

We've been taught to believe that freedom requires something we may not have—a lot of money, abundant leisure, and unfailing self-confidence. Yet many of us found that the real source of freedom comes from within. Bonnie believes that "freedom is making choices. I use *choice* to mean a choice of attitude, too. I learned to consciously choose not to allow the negative thoughts that fuel the anxiety, and to choose instead the thoughts that give me faith in myself."

Freedom is an "inside job." It can't always be registered with gold stars on your victory chart. You can be free even if you sometimes experience pain or anxiety— free to be kind to yourself, free to trust yourself, free to value yourself. Claire says, "I think freedom is a way of living rather than a place to get to. For me freedom comes with accepting and embracing whatever happens and saying, 'Okay, what can I learn from this?' Tomorrow it may mean something else. I think I'll be redefining freedom every moment that I'm alive."

Alicia observes, "All of us have a hidden reserve of strength. Panic forces us to find it. The real opportunity is to reach down and discover that well of strength that allows us to move forward. We can use the knowledge of who we are to help others as well." You don't need to wait until you are a better person, or feel completely confident to contribute your part. Kathy talked on the phone to several people who were homebound and gave them the encouragement to seek treatment. By being willing to reveal herself, she got a perspective on how much she had learned and gained confidence in her own ability. Edward contributed time to his professional community and was surprised to discover how much his efforts were appreciated. As part of her school program, Alicia did an internship working in a bereavement support group for children who had lost a parent. She saw that her own experience with loss enabled her to listen to the children with patience and understanding. Don't underestimate how much your experience and wisdom may mean to others.

Your Bridge

I am grateful that I got the help I needed, that my family and friends were patient with me when I felt frozen and were supportive of me as I gained my independence. I am grateful that I can drive across the Bay Bridge, that I went to India, that I can go places by myself and enjoy being alone. From having panic and phobias, I have learned what gives me peace of mind and makes my life fulfilling. The very bridge that I once dreaded showed me the way to love myself. I am especially grateful to the wonderful people I have met who have opened their hearts to me and told their stories, and to you who are reading these stories and sharing the desire to live fully.

Although each of us can tell you what has contributed to our experience of freedom, you will have to discover freedom for yourself. Explore your own experiences. Document your story. If you haven't already started a journal, begin one now. Make your book beautiful for you. Decorate it, draw pictures on the pages. Cover them with bus transfers and plane tickets, toll slips, photos, school registration cards, and thank-you notes to yourself. Let tears fall on the pages, let anger be recorded, let joy have a voice. Respect your feelings. Respect your process.

Your discovery of freedom need never end because freedom is an active choice each moment to honor your journey. Every time you enter the classroom, go to the store, drive the extra mile, ride to the next station, go up one more floor, make the phone call, share your gifts, speak your truth, treat yourself with kindness, stay a few minutes longer, breathe one more deep breath—you are nurturing the spirit of freedom within you.

On my desk I keep a quote from the famous dancer and choreographer Martha Graham. I first read it several years ago on someone's bulletin board, then saw it on a friend's refrigerator door. Because it has the ring of truth, it has been handed from friend to friend, and now I want to pass it on to you.

> *There is a vitality, a life force, an energy, a quickening that is translated through you into action. And because there is only one of you in all time, this expression is unique. If you block it, it will never exist through any other medium and it will be lost. The world will not have it. It is not your business to determine how good it is, nor how valuable, nor how it compares with other expressions. It is your business to keep it yours clearly and directly, to keep the channel open.*

You are here in the world to express yourself and to find your place in the greater scheme of things. You cannot even imagine what discoveries await you on your journey. You cannot possibly predict what doors will open for you in the months ahead or where you will be years from now. Be a witness to your own self-discovery. There is no more exciting or satisfying adventure.

BIRDWINGS

*Your grief for what you've lost lifts a mirror
up to where you're bravely working.*

*Expecting the worst, you look, and instead,
here's the joyful face you've been wanting
    to see.*

*Your hand opens and closes and opens
    and closes.
If it were always a fist or always
    stretched open,
you would be paralyzed.*

*Your deepest presence is in every small
    contracting and expanding,
the two as beautifully balanced and
    coordinated
as birdwings.*

—Rumi
Translated by Coleman Barks

Epilogue

Although these stories end here, the lives of the people you have met continue to unfold and expand. As of this printing . . .

Howard (Dr. Howard Liebgold) has retired from his position as head of the Department of Rehabilitation at Kaiser Medical Center. When not traveling to some exotic place or going out dancing, he spends his time saving lives by teaching others how to cure phobias and fears the Phobease way. He lectures all over the country and has appeared on several TV shows, including *Oprah*.

Bonnie continues to become more independent as her daughter gets older. She feels more free to move around the world. In the past few years, she has taken several trips to the East Coast and to Europe and has flown home from Hawaii by herself. She has learned to savor life, from playing racquetball with her friends to working peacefully in her garden.

Edward keeps expanding his territory by traveling more often for his work, including trips to southern California and Florida. But his greatest joy is that all the energy he spent worrying is now available to fully engage in every part of his life. He miraculously finds he can be a professional, a husband, and a father, and still make time for his spirit.

Kathy is grateful that she was able to move to a peaceful and beautiful community in a different part of the country. She is meeting new people and doing many of the ordinary things she used to be afraid of, such as taking an evening walk or going shopping. She went to a dentist for the first time in ten years, took visiting friends sightseeing, and even left the car behind and took a one-hour ferry ride to picnic on an island.

Brian has just returned from a two-month trip to East Africa. He spent the first month on a safari and the second traveling by himself to Zanzibar, Mombasa, and Lamu. He went not knowing anyone but met wonderful people all along the way and didn't have one moment of panic.

Alicia completed her graduate program and received a master's degree in counseling psychology. She is seeing her own clients as an intern at a community counseling center. She loves her work and is grateful for her growing ease in engaging with people both in person and on the phone.

Claire feels like she is living her life with open hands and an open heart. Freed from her preoccupation with panic, she has the trust to live in the present moment and to negotiate even her most difficult relationships with honesty and respect. She has given a welcome address to an audience of five hundred people, and turned her attention to her passion for writing poetry.

Resources

The Anxiety and Phobia Peer Support Network

Recognizing that the emotional encouragement and authentic accounts of other people recovering from panic and phobias played a significant role in her healing process, Mani Feniger was inspired to found the Anxiety and Phobia Peer Support Network (APPSN). The network is a telephone support system that matches people who have had positive healing experiences with those seeking understanding and practical feedback to complement the professional guidance or treatment they are receiving.

The APPSN is not a professional organization, a crisis hotline, or a medical referral service. It provides a database through which people who have personally faced the challenges of anxiety can contribute to the well-being of others. If you are seeking additional support, or are willing to share what has helped you cope with anxiety, panic attacks, or phobias, please contact the Anxiety and Phobia Peer Support Network at the following address:

Mani Feniger
Anxiety and Phobia Peer Support Network
P.O. Box 7076
Berkeley, CA 94707
1-888-748-PEER

Other Organizations

The Anxiety Disorders Association of America
11900 Parklawn Dr.
Rockville, MD 20852-2624
(301) 231-9350

Freedom from Fear
308 Seaview Ave.
Staten Island, NY 10305
(718) 351-1717

National Institute of Mental Health
5600 Fishers Lane
Rockville, MD 20857
1-800-64-PANIC

Obsessive-Compulsive Foundation
P.O. Box 70
Milford, CT 06460
(203) 878-5669

Phobics Anonymous
P.O. Box 1180
Palm Springs, CA 92263
(619) 322-COPE

Home Study Tapes and Programs

Attacking Anxiety (16-tape set, workbook)
Midwest Center for Stress and Anxiety
106 N. Church Street, Suite 200
Oak Harbor, OH 43449
(419) 898-4357

CHAANGE (Center for Help for Anxiety/Agoraphobia
   through New Growth Experiences)
128 Country Club Drive
Chula Vista, CA 92011
(619) 425-3992

I Can Do It series by Edmund Bourne, Ph.D.
New Harbinger Publications
5674 Shattuck Avenue
Oakland, CA 94609
1-800-748-6273

Overcoming Phobias (2-tape set, workbook)
Howard Liebgold, M.D.
Kaiser Medical Center
975 Sereno Drive
Vallejo, CA 94547
1-707-651-2297

TERRAP (Territorial Apprehension)
932 Evelyn Street
Menlo Park, CA 94025
1-800-2-PHOBIA

Anxiety to Freedom tapes by Mani Feniger
1-888-748-7337

Newsletters

ENcourage Newsletter
13610 North Scottsdale, Suite 10-126
Scottsdale, AZ 85254

The National Panic/Anxiety Disorder Newsletter
1718 Burgundy Place, Suite B
Santa Rosa, CA 95403
(707) 527-5738

Self-Help Books

The Anxiety and Phobia Workbook, Second edition
by Edmund Bourne, Ph.D.
New Harbinger Publications, Oakland, CA, 1995

Dying of Embarrassment: Help for Social Anxiety &
    Phobia
by Barbara Markway, Ph.D., Cheryl Carmin, Ph.D.,
    C. Alex Pollard, Ph.D., and Teresa Flynn, Ph.D.
New Harbinger Publications, Oakland, CA, 1992

Fly Without Fear
by Carol Stauffer, M.S.W. and Captain F. Petee
Frank Petee & Carol Stauffer Publishers, Pittsburgh,
    PA, 1989

Stop Obsessing!
by Edna Foa, Ph.D. and Reid Wilson, Ph.D.
Bantam, New York, NY, 1991

Special Techniques

Progressive Relaxation

Developing a relaxation response can lower your level of anxiety and is essential to becoming calm and present when faced with an uncomfortable situation. You can read over this script and then do it intuitively from memory, or you can record it on a tape and play it back to yourself. Some people enjoy hearing soothing music in the background.

It is best to do this process regularly, preferably at the same time each day. Reserve fifteen or twenty minutes when you won't be interrupted. It is important to choose a position in which you feel your body is completely supported and which allows the lungs and abdomen to expand without restriction.

Turn down the lights, loosen any tight clothing, and find a comfortable position, either sitting up or lying down. Give your weight over to gravity, letting your body soften and settle upon the chair or cushions. Let your eyes close, and observe your breathing, allowing your

belly to rise and fall with each breath. Now begin the
process of slowly moving your awareness throughout
your body, tensing and relaxing each major muscle
group. Tense your feet by flexing them upward, contract-
ing the muscles in your feet and ankles. Hold this position for 3 or 4 seconds . . . and release . . . Feel your feet
relax, allowing all tension to drain back into the earth . . .
Next, tighten the muscles of your calves and thighs . . .
Hold the tension . . . hold . . . and release . . . Feel the
relief of letting the tension go . . . Take a few deep
breaths . . . Your body knows just what it needs to do to
relax . . . Tighten the muscles of your buttocks and groin
area . . . hold . . . hold . . . and release . . . Now tighten
your stomach and back muscles, pulling the stomach in
toward the back . . . hold the tension . . . hold . . . and
release . . . letting go deeper into relaxation . . . deeper
into calm . . . Raise your arms and make a fist with your
hands . . . hold . . . hold . . . and release . . . Raise your
shoulders up toward the ears . . . hold . . . hold . . . and
release . . . Take a few breaths, allowing the shoulder
blades to move back toward each other as the shoulders
and chest expand and relax . . . melting into the support
of chair or cushion . . . And now tighten the muscles of
your face . . . tense the tiny muscles around your eyes,
forehead, nose, and mouth . . . hold the facial muscles . . .
hold . . . and release . . . Soften your brows . . . melt the
places around your eyes and nose . . . let your jaw open
and slacken . . . allowing your body to rest in the ways it
knows best . . . Breathing in . . . breathing out . . . Letting
your whole body relax . . . Feeling your weight being
supported by the chair (or couch or floor) . . . There is

nothing that needs to happen . . . Letting go . . . naturally . . . releasing . . . resting . . . relaxing.

You may choose to stay a few more moments before you slowly begin to move. Gently stretch your body as you return to awareness of your surroundings, feeling refreshed, relaxed, and renewed. If you have the time, you may choose to stay longer in your relaxation position and imagine yourself in your special place.

Special Place Imagery

Now that you are relaxed, take this opportunity to be in your special place. It may be a location where you have been before, or it may be some place that exists only here in your inner world. It can be indoors or in nature—anywhere you feel safe, comfortable, and at ease. Take another breath and let the qualities of your special place appear into your awareness. Notice the colors and the shapes in your special place. What do you see as you look around you? . . . What do you hear? . . . Describe the smells and sounds of your special place . . . Touch the surfaces and describe the textures of your special place . . . Let it be just the way you want it . . . your place to relax, your special place to be. Enjoy your time here. Stay as long as you wish.

When you are ready, you can leave your special place, knowing it is always here when you want to return. Bring your awareness to your body sitting or lying down. Take a breath. Release it with a long sigh. Stretch your arms and legs. Open your eyes. Stand up slowly and feel the weight of your body supported by your feet and legs. Stretch the crown of your head up toward the ceiling or sky, anchor your feet firmly on the floor or earth. When you are ready, you can continue with your day or evening, knowing your special place is always here in your heart, always available, offering you comfort and calm.

A Guide for Listening to Your Inner Child

1. Envision a special place in your inner world where you and your child self can be alone together. Make it more vivid in your imagination by picturing details, such as colors, furniture, or plants that make you feel comfortable and secure.

2. Invite your inner child to join you here. You may find that with your intention, a picture or sense of this child naturally emerges in your mind's eye. You can also look at a childhood photograph while you do this process or relate to the child from a memory.

3. Gently approach this child and sit down nearby, simply observing his or her appearance—clothing, gestures, and facial expression. You may sense what this child self is feeling, for those feelings are also part of you.

4. Let her or him know that you are the present-day adult. The two of you may communicate by using words, by reaching out a hand, touching a shoulder, or conveying your presence through sensing each other.

5. Invite the child to share whatever he or she is feeling or needs to talk about. You may say something like, "I care about you; I want to get to know you. Is there anything you want to tell me today?" Release any predefined expectations and just observe whatever happens or doesn't happen.

6. Give this child your undivided attention. You don't need to solve any problems, make any decisions, or "raise" this child. Your inner child needs your compassion, patience, and willingness to listen. This is the child's chance to discover that he or she does not have to behave in a particular way to win your love.

7. If your child self is silent, or angry, or afraid, be ready to witness whatever is so. This will begin the process of building inner trust and creating a forum to explore your present feelings in relation to the child's feelings fueled by past memories. Connect to the strength of your compassionate adult by repeatedly returning to the position of witness, saying, "I hear you. Is there anything else?"

8. Spend as long as is natural for you. When you feel ready to finish, let the child know that you can be counted on whenever she or he feels scared, lost, hurt, or unhappy. You may even ask your child self to suggest a signal or word to use to get your attention when there is a need for communication.

9. Notice how you are affected when you listen with respect for your own feelings. Do you feel more comfortable with yourself? Are you willing to let the frightened child rest in your lap when anxiety

arises? Can you make room in your heart for the part of you that sometimes feels small and helpless?

10. Take a deep, refreshing breath, open your eyes, and return to full awareness of your surroundings. When you have finished the process, you can decide if any further action or communication is appropriate.

About the Author

Mani Feniger is a teacher, hypnotherapist, speaker, and writer. In her private practice and workshops, she combines psychological insights and behavioral techniques with respect for the journey of the human spirit. Mani has been a consultant on two documentary films, *Breaking Silence* (1984) and *Stories of Change* (1992). She is the founder of the Anxiety and Phobia Peer Support Network.